HEALTHY EATING
LOW FRUCTOSE

100 recipes to calm the stomach

Authors: Anne Kamp, Christiane Schäfer

Photography: Jörn Rynio

NEW HOLLAND

CONTENTS

FRUCTOSE MALABSORPTION

RECIPES

Breakfast, Spreads and Drinks

Salads

Soups and Snacks

Main Courses

Desserts

Cakes and Baking

LOOK IT UP

FRUCTOSE MALABSORPTION

WHEN FRUCTOSE CAUSES DISCOMFORT

In Western countries approximately 1 in 3 people suffer from sometimes extremely severe digestion problems after ingesting fructose. For many, it has become a daily discomfort because high levels of fructose are now found in many foods, not just fruit.

However, changing your diet quickly and permanently alleviates the symptoms of fructose malabsorption, and this easy-to-follow guide shows you how to successfully do just that. Luckily previous recommendations of avoiding sweets and fruit for the rest of one's life are now a thing of the past.

With selected, low-fructose recipes – especially suitable desserts, pastries and snacks – you can indulge your sweet tooth without worrying about upsetting your stomach. Many practical tips will also help you to prepare your favourite recipes in a low-fructose way, gradually restoring normality to your diet.

FRUCTOSE MALABSORPTION

WHAT IS IT EXACTLY?

THE SUGAR VARIETY KNOWN AS FRUCTOSE (fruit sugar) is naturally present in fruit, fruit juices and some vegetables. Like all other nutrients, it is transported from the small intestine into the blood through the intestinal wall in a process known as resorption or absorption. If this process does not work properly, it is called malabsorption.

The term "fructose malabsorption" thus describes a digestive disorder relating to a specific type of sugar transportation in which the absorption of fructose from the small intestine into the blood is insufficient or dysfunctional. The dietary causes of this disorder have only recently become known, but it is estimated that around 10 percent of all Australians have a limited fructose absorption from the small intestine.

UNSETTLED GUT

Loud tummy rumbles, bloating, flatulence diarrhoea, stomach tension – we all experience these complaints from time to time, but the patients suffering from fructose malabsorption are faced with such discomfort every single day. There is often a list of suspect foods which are sporadically tolerated, and initial examinations by the GP usually find nothing, thus frequently marking the start of a long and frustrating road to determine the cause of the complaints. Once the "culprit" is found, however, a change in diet provides rapid relief.

"SUGAR" IN OUR DIET

Our food is made up of many different components, one of which is carbohydrates. They are the most important source of energy for daily activities and vital processes in the body. In common parlance, "sugar" is usually the collective term for carbohydrate subgroups. But not all sugars are alike. Although most sugars taste "sweet" to us, their chemical structures vary considerably. Most of the foods we eat contain not just one but several different types of sugars, namely monosaccharides and disaccharides (see pages 10–11 for more information). The monosaccharides group also includes the sugar known as fructose.

PENETRATING THE CELLS

The digestion of carbohydrates starts in the mouth, as soon as we have taken a bite or a drink. But most of the work is performed in the duodenum (the upper section of the small intestine) once they have passed through the stomach. The blood in our bodies can only absorb the smallest carbohydrate component, the so-called monosaccharides, or single sugars, which is why the entire digestive process is designed so that the carbohydrates we consume are broken down in the duodenum until only monosaccharides, such as fructose or glucose, are present. In healthy people, they are almost completely absorbed.

THE SPECIAL CASE OF FRUCTOSE

Fructose is absorbed by the so-called GLUT 5 transporter, which transfers it from the small intestine to the body's cells. However, fructose also finds its way into our metabolism through non-active transportation ("passive diffusion"), tagging along with another monosaccharide, such as glucose. Neither transportation mechanism is very effective.

As there are more transportation systems available for all the other monosaccharides, fructose is also always the slowest to be absorbed. Large quantities of over 35 g (1¼ oz) per hour even exceed the absorption capacities of healthy people, causing digestive complaints and consequently diarrhoea. 35 g (1¼ oz) of fructose can be found, for example, in 6 dried figs, half a bag (110 g/4 oz) of raisins or just two glasses (550 ml/18 fl oz/2⅓ cups) of apple juice, but many popular health drinks also have a high fructose content. It is therefore no wonder that a stomach gets upset – even in normally healthy people – after the consumption of dried fruit, fruit juices or other similar drinks.

IMPAIRED TRANSPORTATION OF FRUCTOSE

Even if all the digestive and transportation systems in our gastrointestinal tract are working perfectly, eating large helpings of dried fruit can sometimes still cause bloating, although digestion returns to normal once this wind has passed, or at least after the next bowel movement.

In the case of fructose malabsorption, however, the GLUT 5 transporter's function is severely limited or even non-existent, meaning the fructose that has been consumed can only slip into the body via the passive transportation route. In doing so, part of the fructose stays in the digestive tract and from there advances into the large intestine.

BLOATING AND DIARRHOEA

The constant presence of fructose changes the flora of the bacteria found in the large intestine. They now metabolise the fructose into products such as carbon dioxide (CO_2), hydrogen (H_2) and methane (CH_4), causing bloating and diarrhoea. Short-chain fatty acids (n-butyrate, lactate) are also formed, further softening the stool. This additional volume stimulates bowel movement. Depending on how full the large intestine is, the patient may then suffer from bloating, a feeling of pressure in the upper abdomen, varying stool consistencies (to the point of becoming diarrhoea) and/or colic-like stomach pains.

BEWARE OF SORBITOL!

Sorbitol is a sugar alcohol (see pages 10–11 for an explanation) inhibiting the absorption of fructose in the body, as it uses the same transport routes. Large quantities of sorbitol in food thus further impair absorption of this monosaccharide. Avoid foods containing sorbitol, especially when you first start changing your diet. These foods are shown in the Three-stage plan (see pages 14–15).

POSSIBLE SYMPTOMS OF FRUCTOSE MALABSORPTION

> stomach pains, to the point of becoming stomach cramps
> clearly audible bowel sounds
> bloating
> permanent bloating
> varying stool consistency
> diarrhoea
> constipation
> feeling of pressure in upper abdomen
> abdominal pain
> nausea
> loss of appetite

THE DIAGNOSIS – AN INTOLERANCE

AND HOW TO IDENTIFY IT

YOU MUST MAKE ABSOLUTELY SURE your diagnosis of fructose malabsorption is 100 percent certain before starting to change your diet and avoid anything containing fructose. The hydrogen breath test is essential for ensuring a reliable diagnosis, and cannot be substituted by blood or stool tests. The advantage of breath tests is that they can be conducted safely on all patients, including children.

> Your GP will decide whether or not a hydrogen breath test is required in your case. It is not necessary, for example, for patients with congenital fructose malabsorption, as all fructose intake must be avoided in these cases.

THE HYDROGEN BREATH TEST

The hydrogen breath test measures the concentration of hydrogen (H_2) in exhalation air in ppm (parts per million). Before the measurement is taken, the patient must first drink a fructose solution, then blow into the breathalysing device at regular intervals.

This test takes advantage of the very situation causing the problems – namely the fact that the bacteria present in the gastrointestinal tract metabolise sugar. If fructose cannot be transported properly in the small intestine, or if the amount of fructose consumed exceeds the maximum digestible capacity, the fructose

continues on undigested into the large intestine, where it is fermented by bacteria, producing the fermentation gases hydrogen (H_2) and methane. The H_2 gas gets into the bloodstream through the intestinal wall (diffusion), eventually making its way to the pulmonary alveoli, where it is exhaled (and can thus be measured).

Previously commonly used examinations, such as a colonoscopy, various medications or other underlying diseases, such as bacterial dysbiosis in the intestine, can distort breath test results. Different sugar solutions are used for these patients, for example lactulose or glucose solutions, to further clarify the symptoms. But it's not just the results of the hydrogen breath test which are important. Symptoms occurring during and shortly after the test also provide valuable information. Only after assessing these can it be decided whether or not a change in diet is worthwhile. The hydrogen breath test is thus extremely significant for diagnosing diarrhoea, bloating, nausea and other uncharacteristic digestive tract complaints.

HELP FOR THE GUT

Healthy intestinal flora can be supported by functional foods such as probiotic yoghurts. These functional foods are divided into the subgroups of probiotics and prebiotics. Probiotics or foods containing probiotic components are often recommended for patients suffering from fructose malabsorption, although this recommendation does not apply across the board. You

PROBIOTICS

Probiotic foods contain living micro-organisms which assist gut function and strengthen immunity. Lactobacteria and bifidobacteria are those most commonly used to enhance dairy products.
In order to make the most of such products' benefits, you should consume probiotics daily, as their positive effect is cumulative. The "little helpers" are particularly recommended for those patients also suffering from irritable bowel syndrome, while people with additional lactose intolerance can ask their pharmacy to suggest the lactose-free options to them.

PREBIOTICS

Foods with added prebiotics, such as fructooligosaccharides and inulin, support the natural gut flora and have a positive effect on gut function, but they do contain fructose, which is why they may not benefit people suffering from fructose malabsorption. As no studies have as yet been conducted on this matter, we would dissuade anyone with a fructose intolerance from consuming prebiotics until further research has been conducted.

should test for yourself whether or not these products work well for you. Prebiotics, on the other hand, should be avoided, based on current scientific knowledge (see box in the top right-hand corner).

IMPORTANT!

The fructose malabsorption described here must be clearly distinguished from hereditary fructose intolerance, which is a congenital metabolic disorder.

The table below shows the main differences between these two fundamentally distinct disorders. Patients suffering from hereditary fructose intolerance must follow a completely different diet for their entire lives, and therefore cannot follow the dietary changes and moderate low-fructose food recommendations detailed in this book.

FRUCTOSE MALABSORPTION = ACQUIRED DIGESTIVE DISORDER	DISTINGUISHING FEATURES	HEREDITARY FRUCTOSE INTOLERANCE = CONGENITAL METABOLIC DISORDER
> Disorder affecting the GLUT 5 transporter in the small intestine	> Cause	> Aldolase B enzyme deficiency in the liver
> Often temporary	> Duration of disorder	> Life-long disorder
> Hydrogen breath test	> Diagnosis methods	> Blood test
> Moderate low-fructose food	> Diet	> Strict low-fructose diet for life
> Affects about 30% of people	> Incidence	> Affects <1 in 10,000

MAKING LIFE SWEETER

USING SUGAR CORRECTLY

YOU DON'T HAVE TO GIVE UP sweet things completely just because you suffer from fructose malabsorption. Some types of sugars are tolerated, while others cause problems, which is why a little bit of sugar know-how is generally helpful.

The smallest sugar components are the monosaccharides, or single sugars, which include glucose and fructose. The next group of sugars, the disaccharides, or double sugars, are formed in many different combinations. Saccharose, widely known as household sugar, is produced when a fructose molecule connects with a glucose molecule. Many of these double molecules are interlinked in one single crystal of household sugar. If the saccharose is digested in the small intestine, the fructose becomes a monosaccharide once more, and can cause all the aforementioned problems in people with fructose malabsorption. But fructose can also exist in other sugars. Our small sugar glossary will help you understand product ingredient lists and avoid consuming fructose unknowingly.

GLUCOSE/DEXTROSE is a monosaccharide. It is tolerated very well by people with fructose malabsorption, and improves fructose digestion in the intestine by also working as a "smuggler", making it much easier for the fructose to slip through the intestinal wall. Glucose is thus an ideal sweetener, and is sold as a powder in every supermarket. It can be used as a household sugar substitute to make pastries and desserts – simply replace the household sugar with the glucose. But remember: glucose is 30 percent less sweet than household sugar, so you will actually need 30 percent more glucose than the amount of household sugar stated in the recipe.

CARBOHYDRATE	TOLERABILITY
MONOSACCHARIDES	
Glucose	☺
Fructose (fruit sugar)	☹
DISACCHARIDES	
Saccharose (household sugar) = glucose + fructose	☺ ☹
Lactose (milk sugar) = glucose + galactose	☺
Maltose (malt sugar) = glucose + glucose	☺

It is particularly important to use glucose in the initial abstention phase. Once your symptoms have abated, it can be re-substituted with household sugar. Too much glucose (over 100 g/3⅓ oz per hour) causes digestive problems even in healthy people, so only eat standard-size servings of dishes in which it has been used as a sweetener. Glucose syrup is predominantly made from glucose, and is tolerated without any problem.

RICE SYRUP essentially comprises glucose and maltose, making it ideal for people with fructose malabsorption.

FRUCTOSE is also a monosaccharide, found in all fruits and some vegetables. Fruit juices and dried fruit are particularly rich in fructose, containing more of this sugar than other monosaccharides. Fructose is very often used in large quantities in diabetic foods. It also occasionally serves as an additive in the food industry, appearing as fructose syrup on ingredients lists, which is why such lists need to be scrutinised very carefully. Foods rich in fructose should be avoided particularly during the first or abstention phase of the Three-stage diet. Apart from fruit, the largest source of fructose in our diet is household sugar (see below).

SACCHAROSE is the chemical name for household sugar. It is part of the disaccharides group made up of glucose and fructose, and is extracted from sugar beets or sugar cane. During the abstention period, avoid household sugar and instead replace it with glucose. Depending on the severity of the fructose malabsorption, some patients can tolerate small quantities of household sugar. However, you should only test your personal tolerance threshold once the first phase is complete and you have virtually no more symptoms. Saccharose is also contained in the following products: brown sugar, jam setting sugar, coarse sugar crystals, rock candy, granulated/refined sugar, icing sugar, raw sugar, vanilla sugar, industrial sugar.

INVERT SUGAR (artificial honey) is a mixture of glucose and fructose, and should be avoided at the start of the diet.

LACTOSE (milk sugar) is formed as a disaccharide made from glucose and galactose, and it is predominantly found in milk and dairy products such as curd cheese, yoghurt and cream, as well as some ready-made products. Cheese – particularly harder varieties like Cheddar, Emmental and Gouda – and butter contain only small quantities. Lactose is tolerated without any problem.

MALTOSE (malt sugar) exists as a disaccharide comprising two parts glucose, that is it is made entirely of glucose, meaning it is very well tolerated.

MALTODEXTRIN is a polysaccharide made up of four to five parts glucose, and is also very well tolerated.

It has barely any sweet taste and is often used instead as a stabiliser, filler and preservative. Maltodextrin can be found in ready-made soup mixes, meats and sausages, sweets and baby food.

MAPLE SYRUP, APPLE SYRUP, PEAR SYRUP and **HONEY** are all made of up to 80 percent various sugars – some, of course, containing significant amounts of fructose. These foods should thus be avoided during the abstention phase.

SWEETENERS are manufactured synthetically and are practically calorie-free. Chemically, they are not sugars, and are thus tolerated very well by people suffering from fructose malabsorption. **SACCHARIN, ASPARTAME, CYCLAMATE, ACESULPHAME POTASSIUM** and **THAUMATIN** are sweeteners that are permitted by law in Australia. They all taste sweet, with 300 to 500 times more sweetness than household sugar.

SUGAR SUBSTITUTES (sugar alcohols) are mostly used by the food industry. They have the advantage of tasting sweet without causing any dental cavities, and are therefore frequently found in chewing gum and lollies labelled as being "sugar free".

Sugar substitutes are also widely used in diabetic sweets. If consumed in excess, they tend to have a laxative effect even in healthy people. Those suffering from fructose malabsorption should ideally avoid all sugar alcohols so as not to place an additional strain on the already irritated gut. The group of sugar alcohols comprises sorbitol (E 420), mannitol (E 421), isomalt (E 953), maltitol (E 965), lactitol (E 966) and xylitol (E 967).

IT'S THAT EASY

THREE STEPS TO A SETTLED STOMACH

IF YOU HAVE BEEN DIAGNOSED with fructose malabsorption, the first step has already been taken. You can now start actively changing your diet over three phases – and it's easier than you think. If you're having trouble making the change yourself, contact an experienced dietitian.

PHASE 1 (ABSTENTION PHASE)

During this phase, you should only eat the foods that are listed in the left-hand column of the table (see pages 14–15). The phase table (see front flap) contains numerous dishes you can eat during this time.

The foods consumed as part of this dietary phase are strictly low in fructose. Those containing fructose and sorbitol are avoided almost entirely (abstention). This period normally lasts between two and four weeks, and ends only once the symptoms have noticeably eased. If you have had virtually no symptoms for five consecutive days, you can move into the second phase.

Sufficient fluid intake is now particularly important: Adults must drink at least 2 litres (70 fl oz/8½ cups) a day, and children at least 1.5 litres (60 fl oz/7½ cups). Still mineral water and herbal tea are ideal drinks. Carbonated beverages unnecessarily generate air in the digestive tract. Foods known to cause flatulence and bloating, such as cabbage, onions and pulses, have a negative effect on the healing process.

Take your time when eating, being sure to chew everything properly. This will help settle your gut. You should also inform your friends and family; children often eat the wrong thing because their grandparents have fed them sweets. Children should also wait until they have had no symptoms for at least five days before starting the second phase. If symptoms have still not eased after two to four weeks of following the abstention phase diet, check your diet for incorrect foods. If in doubt, consult your dietitian or doctor.

PHASE 2 (TEST PHASE)

Your gut will have noticeably settled, and you're feeling much better overall. In this phase, you will test out foods from the middle column of the table (see pages 14–15). These foods contain moderate amounts of fructose and are tolerated well in standard-sized serves. The foods in the left-hand column continue to form the basis of your diet, but they are now being enhanced and complemented by the foods listed in the middle column. The phase table (see front flap) contains an overview of dishes suitable for the test phase. You can also keep enjoying the recipes suggested for the abstention period.

Only ever try out new foods in small serves. If symptoms reappear after consumption, initially avoid the food and test out something else from the middle column. This way you will gradually find out which foods your gut can currently tolerate. Tolerability often improves after a few months so you can always test the earmarked foods again at another time.

Fructose-containing foods which you eat in the morning on an empty stomach are not as well tolerated as those you eat later during the day, for example after lunch. So it is preferable to test the "new" foods and drinks later in the day.

When testing dishes that have been prepared using household sugar – cakes, biscuits or ice cream for example – eat 1 teaspoon of glucose or 1 small glucose tablet at the same time. This will improve the glucose-to-fructose ratio. If you are able to tolerate the dish well, you can try it again later without the glucose. Start off with small serves; that way you will be able to tell quickly how much fructose your gut can take each day. Many people suffering from fructose malabsorption find they can tolerate small daily serves of sugary foods (one piece of cake, two to four biscuits or two scoops of ice cream) in the longterm.

You should exercise caution when eating foods which are harder to digest, for example grainy wholemeal bread or cabbage. Similarly onions and pulses should only be introduced very gradually – they often cause stomach rumbles or bloating even in healthy people. So if you hear your gut making a few noises after eating these foods, it doesn't mean you've made a mistake. If it tastes good and is well tolerated, you can reintroduce the relevant food item into your daily diet.

Keep a food journal (see page 23 for a sample of how to lay one out) during the test phase, listing all the food and drinks you have consumed, as well as any symptoms which appear. This is the best way to accurately determine your personal tolerability threshold.

Fast, hasty eating and inadequate chewing can also cause stomach upsets, while stress and anxiety most certainly affect our digestion. Daily relaxation exercises and walks sometimes work wonders – and are particularly important for people in primarily sedentary jobs. Build a 30-minute walk into your daily routine.

The test phase lasts for one to two months, and then runs into the third and final phase, the longterm diet phase.

PHASE 3 (LONGTERM DIET)

You have gained enough experience with different fructose quantities and developed a sense of how much you can tolerate. However, you should still ensure sufficient nutrient intake, despite the restrictions imposed on your fruit and vegetable intake. The recommended quantity for adults is approximately 500 g (1 lb) of vegetables and 250–300 g (8–10 oz) of fruit per day. Primary-school children should eat 300 g (10 oz) of vegetables and one to two fruits per day. Experience has shown that bananas are often well tolerated.

You should also test out the other fruits in the middle column (see pages 14–15). If they are tolerated, regularly build small quantities of these into your diet. If, however, your gut cannot tolerate this amount of fructose, you should counterbalance these with an adequate quantity of vegetables. Capsicums, radishes, cucumbers and possibly even carrots are an ideal snack rich in vitamins, ensuring an appropriate nutrient intake.

Foods high in fructose should only be avoided for as long as absolutely necessary, because they also provide valuable vitamins, minerals and secondary plant substances.

THE THREE-STAGE PLAN – FRUCTOSE-FRIENDLY FOOD AND DRINK

	Diet phase 1 – ABSTENTION PHASE – low in fructose always suitable	Diet phase 2 – TEST PHASE – modified fructose levels suitable to a limited extent	Symptoms caused by excess fructose not suitable
Drinks	**Water:** non-carbonated mineral water, tap water **Non-alcoholic drinks:** calorie-free so-called "light" drinks (e.g. iced tea, lemonade with sweetener) **Coffee and tea:** ground coffee, green and black tea (maximum 4 cups a day), fruit and herbal teas (tisanes) **Alcohol:** pils-style beers, clear schnapps	**Water:** lightly carbonated mineral water **Non-alcoholic drinks:** lemonade, coke, fruit juice spritzers (from the fruit varieties listed in this column), vegetable juices, iced tea **Coffee and tea:** instant coffee, instant tea powder **Alcohol:** wheat beer, malt beer, herb liqueur, liqueur, dry wines	**Non-alcoholic drinks:** health drinks containing fructose/sorbitol/isomalt; fruit juices, fruit cocktails (both with and without alcohol) **Alcohol:** fortified wines, late harvest wines
Vegetables and vegetable products	eggplant, celery, cucumber, cabbages (cauliflower*, broccoli*, kohlrabi*, Chinese cabbage*), pumpkin, silverbeet, carrot (in small quantities), olives, capsicum (red and yellow), parsnips, mushrooms (cooked), beetroot, celeriac, asparagus, spinach, tomato (fresh), turnip, zucchini	leafy salad (all kinds), beans (green), chicory, fennel, cabbages (kale*, Brussels sprouts, red cabbage, sauerkraut, cabbage, Savoy cabbage*), kohlrabi, garlic, sweetcorn, capsicum (green), leek, salsify, tomatoes (tinned), snow peas, onions **Plus:** ready-made or semi-prepared foods	artichoke, mushrooms (raw) **Plus:** tinned foods containing fructose or sorbitol
Pulses	peas (green, tinned), soy products (soy milk, tofu etc)	beans (red and white), peas, lentils, yellow beans, soy milk light	broad beans, Lima beans, soy beans (fresh)
Potatoes	potatoes, potato dishes (e.g. French fries, pancakes), potato chips		
Fruit and fruit products	avocado, banana (possibly with dextrose), lychee, papaya, rhubarb (with dextrose or sweetener)	pineapple, apricot, berries (strawberry, blueberry, elderberry, redcurrant, gooseberry), clementine, grapefruit, honeydew melon, kiwi fruit, mandarines, peach, morello cherry, watermelon **Plus:** jelly and jam made from suitable fruits	apple, pear, date, fig, mango, plum, grape, dried fruit (e.g. sultanas) **Plus:** juices, jams or fruit spreads containing fructose, sorbitol or isomalt
Nuts and seeds	nuts (all kinds), coconut, seeds (all kinds)		
Cereals, bread, baked goods, pasta, processed foods	**Cereals:** wheat flour, rye flour (in small quantities), rolled oats, amaranth, buckwheat, spelt, barley, millet, corn, quinoa, wheat bran, couscous, bulgur	**Cereals:** cereal sprouts **Bread and baked goods:** coarse wholemeal bread, bread roll with sugar, honey or syrup, chocolate rolls; cakes, biscuits and baked good containing household sugar; pastries with sugar,	**Muesli and muesli bars:** with dried fruits, with Fructose, sorbitol, Isomalt **Plus:** diabetic baked goods and pastries

* better tolerated when frozen

	Diet phase 1 – ABSTENTION PHASE – low in fructose always suitable	Diet phase 2 – TEST PHASE – modified fructose levels suitable to a limited extent	Symptoms caused by excess fructose not suitable
	Bread and baked goods: bread of finely ground wholemeal flour, bread rolls, croissants, pretzels, mixed-grain bread, white bread, pastries containing glucose **Processed foods:** pasta, rice, unsugared puffed rice, rice waffles **Plus:** cornflakes with maltose or malt	honey or syrup **Muesli:** coarse muesli flakes without fruits; ready-made muesli (e.g. Toasted Muesli) **Plus:** cornflakes, puffed rice with sugar or honey	
Milk and dairy products	milk, mixed milk drink with pure cocoa (without sugar), cream, cream cheese, natural yoghurt (without prebiotic additives), buttermilk, kefir, whey (without fruit additives), unsweetened condensed milk **Cheese:** cream cheese, spreads, semi-hard/soft/hard cheese	fruit yoghurt, fruit whey drinks, sweetened condensed milk, cocoa drink powder with sugar	
Meat and cold meats	**Meat** (all kinds) **Cold meats:** ham and other meats (e.g. turkey breast)	deli meats and seafood products containing sugar/sweetener	
Fish and seafood	**Fish** (all kinds) **Crustaceans** (all kinds)	tinned fish with sugar/sweetener (e.g. herring in tomato sauce)	
Eggs	any kind (e.g. fried, scrambled)	egg dishes sweetened with sugar (e.g. crêpes)	
Fats and oils	all plant and animal fats		
Sugar and sweeteners	**Monosaccharides:** glucose, dextrin, dextrose, glucose syrup **Disaccharides or polysaccharides:** maltose (malt sugar), maltodextrin, lactose (milk sugar), rice syrup **Sweeteners:** saccharin, cyclamate, aspartame	**Disaccharides:** household sugar (saccharose) in all forms, i.e. brown sugar, raw sugar, crystallised sugar, icing sugar, vanilla sugar; maple syrup; glucose-fructose-syrup, cane juice	**Monosaccharides:** fructose, fructose syrup **Sugar substitutes:** sorbitol, xylitol, mannitol, isomalt, maltitol, lactitol **Plus:** apple syrup, pear syrup, honey
Sweets and snacks	glucose lollies salted pretzel sticks, corn puffs, chips, rice cakes	fruity lollies, fruit gum, liquorice, toffees, nougat, pralines, chocolate, marshmallows, marzipan, nut nougat cream	lollies and chocolates containing fructose, sorbitol or isomalt **Plus:** sugar-free chewing gums and lollies
Spices, flavourings and other foods	all herbs and spices; vinegar (except balsamic), mustard (hot and medium), mayonnaise; stock, yeast; vanilla seeds, artificial flavourings; baking powder, gelatine, jelly crystals, unsweetened custard powder	tomato sauce, balsamic vinegar, sweet mustard, condiments, natural flavours (lemon zest, lemon juice), instant custard powder	fruit sauces

DINING OUT

FRUCTOSE TRAPS AND HOW TO AVOID THEM

YOU WILL REALLY NOTICE the supposed "bans" on some of your favourite foods when you first change your diet, but don't be discouraged. The reward for consistently implementing a dietary change is that you can also try out and tolerate food from the test phase relatively easily and quickly.

Don't hesitate to dine out, even during the abstention period. The following dishes can be eaten without any problem:

> all meat and fish dishes (with the exception of any meals containing fruits or Asian-style sweet-and-sour dishes)
> all potato, rice and pasta dishes
> vegetable dishes without foods that are generally known to cause heavy bloating, such as onions, cabbage and pulses
> soups (with the exception of lentil, pea and bean soups)
> small side salads

FOOD	HIDDEN TROUBLEMAKER
> fruit yoghurt	> fruit and considerable quantities of fructose
> horseradish sauce/cream	> apple
> raw vegetable salads	> apple or apple juice
> muesli	> dried fruits
> toasted muesli	> baked with fructose or honey
> red cabbage salad	> apple
> salad dressings	> fructose
> sports or iso-drinks	> large quantities of fructose
> sweet'n'sour chicken	> apple or apple juice
> Waldorf salad	> fruits
> fitness drinks	> large quantities of fructose
> sugar-free chewing gum	> a major source of sugar replacement products and therefore usually laxative. The chewing also leads to swallowing a lot of air which increases discomfort.
> foods claiming "without granulated/household sugar"	> sugar substitutes, usually with fructose and sugar alcohols
> cough syrup, mouth wash, medicine	> sorbitol

If, however, you do find yourself eating a dish quite rich in fructose, you can quickly neutralise the situation by adding glucose. Simply take one glucose tablet during or immediately prior to the meal. This improves the glucose/fructose ratio in the gut, thereby increasing tolerability. It's a good idea to always take a packet of glucose tablets with you as a precaution when dining out, even with friends.

Avoid large serves. A diet with four to five small meals per day makes it easier for your body to process the amount of fructose consumed. If you don't want to skip dessert, just bring a banana from home. It will satisfy your sweet tooth and simultaneously supply you with vitamins and minerals.

When choosing a drink, it is a good idea to consult the table on pages 14–15. Sugary drinks such as lemonade cause problems particularly quickly, as they race straight to the gut and rapidly overwhelm it. A glass of mineral water instead of lemonade protects the gut and also avoids unnecessary calories.

BEWARE OF HIDDEN TROUBLEMAKERS!

It is usually small mistakes which unsettle the stomach. Make sure you read the ingredient lists on any packaging, and do not hesitate to ask questions if in doubt. We have listed some common traps found in supermarkets, restaurants as well as in pharmacies in the table on page 16. Some of these products contain surprisingly large quantities of fructose or sorbitol.

SWEET TOOTH? NOT A PROBLEM!

Glucose lollies are a well-tolerated alternative for satisfying your sweet tooth, even when you are first changing your diet. They are available from supermarkets or chemist shops. Flavoured glucose lollies will not cause you any problems; the added fruit flavours are fructose-free and easily tolerated. The recipe section (see page 90 onwards) contains a further selection of

delicious sweets, pastries and ice creams, allowing you to sweeten up your life once in a while without too much worry. If your symptoms have eased and you have moved into the second phase of the dietary change, you can also start trying small quantities of "normal" sweets from the supermarket. A bar of chocolate, some licorice or fruit gums, for example, can be tolerated well by most people with fructose malabsorption.

However, do not relent and still keep checking the labels whenever you shop. The order of ingredients on the list will provide you with valuable information on their quantities, helping you determine whether the product contains a lot or a little fructose.

SAMPLE INGREDIENTS LISTS

GUMMY BEARS

Ingredients: glucose syrup, sugar, fruit flavouring, gelatine, acidifiers etc.

> Easier to tolerate for people with fructose malabsorption, as the percentage of glucose is higher than the percentage of fructose.

CHEWY LOLLIES, E.G. FRUIT CHEWS

Ingredients: sugar, fructose, glucose syrup, fruit flavouring, gelatine, acidifiers etc.

> Harder to tolerate for people with fructose malabsorption, as the percentage of fructose is higher than the percentage of glucose.

A TIP FOR CHOCOLATE FANS

Dark chocolate with a particularly high percentage of cocoa (at least 70%) contains less sugar than milk chocolate, and is thus easier to tolerate. However, you should remember that this chocolate also contains more fat, so its calorie content is no lower. Anyone who is suffering from lactose intolerance at the same time as fructose malabsorption can also eat this chocolate without any problems, because it is usually dairy/lactose-free. But you should still always check the ingredients list first.

FRUCTOSE UNDER CONTROL

I STILL HAVE A FEW QUESTIONS...

FOR HOW LONG DO I HAVE TO CHANGE MY DIET?

The first phase (abstention) of dietary change lasts two to four weeks. If the symptoms have noticeably abated, you can start adding foods from the second phase (test) to your diet. The test phase usually lasts four to eight weeks, leading into the third or longterm diet phase. The foods from the right-hand column of the table (see pages 14–15) are generally not as well tolerated, although small quantities can normally be ingested without any problems two to three months after changing your diet. Try it out for yourself.

WHAT HAPPENS IF I ACCIDENTALLY EAT THE WRONG THING?

Mistakes are part of human nature, and are not dangerous. As long as you only eat meals that are high in fructose on rare occasions and then alleviate the symptoms by consistently adopting the correct diet, the only side effects you will have to tolerate will be stomach ache, bloating and diarrhoea – in short, the things you had to cope with before you started the diet.

WHY ARE MY SYMPTOMS SOMETIMES WORSE THAN OTHER TIMES?

The most common reason is the amount of fructose eaten. Excessively large meals, eating too quickly, and not drinking enough fluid will also intensify the symptoms, however, as will mental strains such as anxiety and stress. If you cannot work out the cause of your symptoms, keep a food journal (see page 23) for a few days, noting down any symptoms. Even if this does not tell you anything, it will be of great help to your doctor or dietitian.

ARE THE DIETARY RECOMMENDATIONS THE SAME FOR EVERYONE WITH FRUCTOSE MALABSORPTION?

No. Although the Three-stage plan divides the foods into those containing fructose and those low in fructose, it does not note individual intolerances, that is, distinguish between foods which cause more of a "stomach ache" for you personally. These factors must be taken into account and a dietitian can help you with this. The Three-stage plan is, however, recommended for everyone with fructose malabsorption, even if only a slight intolerance is suspected.

WHY IS FRUCTOSE MALABSORPTION BECOMING MORE PREVALENT IN SOCIETY?

Many experts suspect this is due to the fact that people's eating habits – and particularly those of children – are changing drastically, prompting a change in the selection of foods available. Fructose is thus being added much more frequently than in previous decades. However, fructose malabsorption can also be caused by insufficient digestion or intestinal disorders. Doctors and dietitians themselves have only become aware of this intolerance in recent years.

DO MODERN-DAY FOODS PLAY A ROLE IN THE DEVELOPMENT OF FRUCTOSE MALABSORPTION?

Modern-day foods, including health drinks and sugar-free sweets, definitely play a role. Careless selection can result in large amounts of fructose being consumed during a meal. Even healthy food containing lots of fruit can sometimes well exceed the quantities suitable for fructose digestion. Consumption of sweets – and therefore also fructose intake – has similarly risen drastically in recent years.

DOES FRUCTOSE MALABSORPTION CAUSE SERIOUS HEALTH PROBLEMS?

If fructose malabsorption goes untreated, that is, no dietary change is made, the symptoms intensify and digestive function can become increasingly impaired. The natural gut flora, particularly in the large intestine, can become unbalanced due to the arrival of excessively large quantities of fructose. It is assumed that sugar stimulates the growth of substances causing decay and fermentation, which can further worsen symptoms in general.

SHOULD I WORRY ABOUT DEFICIENCY SYMPTOMS?

With the Three-stage plan, we propose a dietary treatment which minimises restrictions to those absolutely necessary. After the low-fructose food in the initial phase, lots more food is re-introduced in the second phase, so you don't have to worry about your nutrient balance. Consult a dietitian in order to avoid longterm nutrient deficiencies (see page 124).

IS FRUCTOSE MALABSORPTION A LIFELONG DISORDER?

There is no conclusive answer to this question, as the symptoms have only become known in recent years. It is suspected, however, that fructose malabsorption can occur temporarily and over the longterm. Past experience has shown that growing children in particular only suffer from it temporarily. Adults, on the other hand, are more likely to suffer lifelong intolerances to large quantities of fructose.

GOOD FOOD AND A GOOD MOOD

TARGETED SUPPORT

EVEN PEOPLE WITH FRUCTOSE malabsorption, who can only eat a limited range of foods, can have an adequate intake of nutrients. The reduced selection of fruit and vegetables available when the diet is first changed does not normally cause any longterm nutrient deficiencies. It is only when there is a combination of several food intolerances involving extremely limited diets that any notable deficiency occurs. The mineral zinc and the vitamin folic acid are particularly important here.

ZINC

A study has shown that 10 percent of all people with fructose malabsorption suffer from a zinc deficiency, particularly evidenced by impaired wound healing, hair loss, heightened susceptibility to infection, and loss of appetite. This very frequently affects people who are also taking hormones. As this study is so far the only one available, we advise against self-medication and taking general zinc supplements if you have fructose malabsorption.

It is instead better to prevent and combat a possible zinc deficiency in the longterm, and regularly eat foods that are rich in this mineral such as meats, dairy products, pulses, wholemeal bread and dark chocolate. Consult your doctor if you are unsure about whether or not you have a zinc deficiency. A simple blood test will give you the answer. Clinically proven zinc deficiencies require medical treatment.

FOLIC ACID

Once again, there is so far only one study available, which states that female patients over 35 who suffer from fructose malabsorp-tion may have lower levels of folic acid in their blood. However, it is also known that 80 percent of people tend to consume insufficient amounts of folic acid. Increasing folic acid intake is thus a general recommendation for everyone – not just people with fructose malabsorption. Foods rich in folic acid include wheatgerm, nuts and wholemeal products. There is not yet any conclusive evidence to state whether, and to what extent, sufficient folic acid intake might affect fructose malabsorption.

A folic acid deficiency is not immediately noticeable, but if it persists over a longer period of time it can cause cardiovascular diseases, as well as deformities in newborns. Once again, you should have your folic acid levels checked by your doctor, and systematically add this vitamin to your diet if necessary.

DEPRESSION

It's not just the body that needs to be well fed and watered – sometimes the mind too sends out a cry for help. It is suspected that patients with fructose malabsorption have a tendency to be depressive, possibly due to modified metabolic processes. Detailed studies have not yet been conducted on this topic, but many people with fructose malabsorption spend months or even years of suffering before being correctly diagnosed, or even being aware of their own unhappiness within themselves. It is no big surprise then that this causes mood swings and even depression.

IF THE STOMACH SIMPLY CANNOT SETTLE

If both an accurate and exact diagnosis and consistent dietary changes still fail to produce the desired results and a relief in symptoms, doubts usually start to creep in.

This is where the analysis of food journals by a dietitian specialising in food intolerances and gastrointestinal disorders can often be of assistance. In ambiguous cases, the food journals quickly show any small, hidden errors and wrong assumptions, which,

when combined, can most certainly be the cause of your symptoms.

Fluid intake is a major cause of unexplained symptoms. Drink at least 2 litres (70 fl oz/8½ cups) of liquid throughout the day. Excessive or inadequate dietary fibre intake frequently also leads to persistent stomach complaints. In general, it is advisable to thoroughly check your personal eating habits if you experience ongoing symptoms, and perhaps consult a health professional.

If, despite all recommendations, the symptoms do not disappear, it may be likely that another undiagnosed digestive tract disorder is present. Please consult your doctor in order to clarify whether or not this is the case.

DISORDER	COMMON SYMPTOM TRIGGERS
> Lactose intolerance	> Milk and dairy products
> Food allergy	> Various foods can cause symptoms in allergic patients as well as in the digestive tract. These often include: milk, egg, soy and wheat in children; hazelnuts, raw stone fruit, pomaceous fruit (such as apples, pears) and kiwi fruit in adults.
> Pancreatic insufficiency	> Symptoms after almost all meals, but particularly after dishes high in fat and sugar
> Intestinal dysbiosis	> Symptoms (e.g. bloating, stomach ache, diarrhoea) after almost all meals, but particularly after dishes high in fat and sugar
> Gallstones	> Symptoms (e.g. stomach ache, cramps) particularly after fatty meals
> Histamine intolerance	> Red wine, mature cheese, tinned fish
> Irritable bowel syndrome	> The exact causes are still unclear, but may include coffee, stress and low fluid intake, among other factors.

A LIFE WITHOUT SYMPTOMS

OTHER THINGS TO REMEMBER

HALF THE DIGESTIVE PROCESS is in the chewing: Anything not ground down in the mouth must be digested by the digestive fluids in the gastrointestinal tract, which is hard work for a weakened gut. Hasty eating often causes the formation of gas, even in people with healthy, robust intestines. So take your time when eating – at least 20 minutes for a main meal. You will soon notice that you tolerate a lot of foods much better if you eat your meals slowly.

SEVERAL SMALL MEALS: Do not unnecessarily overwhelm your gut with huge serves. It is better to eat four to five small meals a day rather than two or three large ones. These will ideally be small snacks containing well-tolerated fruit, plain yoghurt with fruit spread (see pages 30–31), milk with oat flakes, or even a sweet pastry (see page 106 onwards). Bulky and fibrous foods such as leafy salads or raw vegetables are a real challenge for weakened guts – only eat these in small portions, especially at the start.

FATTY DESSERTS ARE MORE EASILY TOLERATED: Many people with fructose malabsorption can tolerate chocolate, ice cream or cake better than ice blocks and lemonade. A high fat content prolongs the time that the fructose spends in the stomach, delaying its arrival in the lower digestive tract and causing hardly any problems. Hearty, savoury meals, however, must be eaten in moderation because large quantities of fat place additional strain on a weakened digestive system.

FROZEN CABBAGE IS EASIER TO DIGEST THAN FRESH: Cabbage contains substances which are well known to cause bloating even in many healthy people. Cauliflower, broccoli and cabbage are all tolerated noticeably better if they have been frozen first. Patients with an extreme tendency to form gas should initially avoid any type of cabbage, and only slowly start incorporating frozen cabbage into their diet once their stomach has settled again.

DRINK LOTS: Sufficient fluid intake helps the gut and encourages healthy stools. Adults should drink 2 litres (70 fl oz/8½ cups) a day and children 1.5 (60 fl oz/7½ cups). However, heavily carbonated beverages should be avoided, particularly in the early phase. This also applies for people with a tendency to feel bloated. The table for the Three-stage plan (see pages 14–15) contains a list of suitable beverages. One simple trick will ensure you never forget to drink – always have a glass of water or cup of tea handy.

EXCESSIVELY HARD STOOL: Is your stool too hard? Then first check your fluid intake. Stewed vegetables and fine-grain wholemeal bread will also help get a lethargic gut going. If you are often constipated it is important to avoid taking laxatives regularly, because this causes important minerals to be lost, and it will also damage the intestinal flora.

FOOD JOURNAL – SAMPLE PAGE

NAME: DATE:

TIME	QUANTITY	FOOD/DRINK	SYMPTOM/STOOL
7.00	1	cup of coffee with milk	
	1	bread roll with butter and cheese	
7.30			stool (normal)
10.00	1	glass orange juice	
11.00			bowel sounds, slight bloating
12.30	1	lasagne, cream cheese with dextrose	
15.00	1	banana	
18.30	2 slices	wholemeal bread with butter and ham	
	2	tomatoes	
21.00	about 25	salty snacks	
	1 bottle	beer	

EXCESSIVELY SOFT STOOL: If your stool is too soft, eat 2 tablespoons of oat flakes stirred in with 1 bowl of plain yoghurt three times a day. This improves stool quality, particularly in the early phase. If, after 2 weeks, your stool is still very soft or you still feel bloated, it means there are still flaws somewhere in your diet. Perhaps you could also be suffering from other undiagnosed disorders or food intolerances. If you regularly experience diarrhoea, make sure you strictly follow the Three-stage plan and discuss further diagnostic measures with your dietitian.

EXERCISE IS RELAXING: Daily walks or other forms of "gentle" exercise help settle the gut. You have no time for a walk? It often just takes a few small changes to your everyday routine in order to get significantly more regular exercise: don't park your car right outside your workplace; walk the last 500 metres instead. Take the stairs instead of the lift. Stand up or, if possible, walk around while making telephone calls. You'll soon notice that regular exercise also destresses and can improve your mood considerably.

REST, FUN AND RELAXATION: Stress causes digestive problems in a vast number of people. For someone with a gut weakened through fructose malabsorption, stress can be the last straw, which is why it is particularly important to include rest and relaxation in everyday routines. Think about what you really enjoy doing, and which situations make you feel particularly good. Take up a new and fulfilling hobby, something you always wanted to do. It may be dancing, painting, singing or reading. You could try out a new sport, join a fitness club or learn a new language. Put into place aplan for enjoying yourself more often and make it a priority!

COOKING, BAKING AND ENJOYING

LOW FRUCTOSE

Enjoy and feast to your heart's content.
The following pages contain a wide selection of
quick, easy and delicious recipes suitable for
all occasions, allowing your stomach to gradually
settle and let you enjoy life once more.

Our recipes are fun for people of all ages to prepare.
Go wild trying out all the cakes, ice creams, desserts and
confectionery – no one has to deprive themselves of sweets. But
don't forget to also test our savoury dishes. They're quick and
simple to prepare and add variety to your weekly diet, allowing even
busy professionals to enjoy tasty, fructose-friendly meals and a life
free from symptoms.

Oatmeal Muesli

SERVES 2

3 tbsp pumpkin seeds

8 tbsp instant oats

500 g (1 lb) yoghurt (3.5% fat)

1 pinch of orange essence
(alternatively 1 pinch of grated zest
of an organic orange)

1 banana

1 tsp dextrose

PREPARATION: about 5 mins

1. Roughly chop 2 tablespoons pumpkin seeds. Set aside 1 teaspoon. Stir the instant oats into the yoghurt, then fold in the chopped seeds and the orange essence.

2. Peel and slice the banana, then fold the slices into the yoghurt mixture.

3. Sweeten the muesli to taste with dextrose and divide it between two breakfast bowls. Sprinkle with the remaining pumpkin seeds.

A GENTLE START

This muesli contains easily digested dietary fibre and is therefore a good way to start a new diet. Instant oats in particular are often better tolerated than rolled oats during the abstention phase. In the second phase of the diet, the so-called test phase, you can also vary your muesli by including any fruits of your choice.

NUTRITIONAL VALUES PER PORTION:

435 Cal • 18 g protein • 19 g fat • 48 g carbohydrate

Toasted Muesli

SERVES 2

125 g (4 oz) porridge oats
30 g (1 oz) sunflower seeds
1 heaped tbsp desiccated coconut
2 tbsp sunflower oil
50 g (1²/₃ oz) dextrose
PREPARATION: about 40 mins

1. Combine the porridge oats, the sunflower seeds and the coconut. Preheat the oven to 150°C/130°C fan-forced (middle shelf). Line a baking tray with baking paper.

2. In a frying pan heat the oil and the dextrose over high heat, stirring constantly, until both combine to form a clear liquid. Sprinkle in the dry ingredients. Cook, stirring, until the oil and sugar mixture has been completely absorbed and the base of the frying pan is dry.

3. Distribute the mixture evenly over the baking tray and roast in the oven for about 20–25 minutes until golden, turning several times while cooking. Lift the muesli off the tray together with the baking paper and leave to cool completely.

TIP

Many ready-made mueslis contain fructose syrup or dried fruits. This basic mix allows you to create your very own toasted breakfast cereal. For a change you could prepare your muesli with nuts, sesame seeds or other cereal flakes. You could also stir 1 teaspoon ground cinnamon into the mixture before roasting. If stored in a well-sealed jar the muesli will stay fresh and crunchy for about 4 weeks.

NUTRITIONAL VALUES PER PORTION:
540 Cal • 12 g protein • 27 g fat • 63 g carbohydrate

Wheat Muesli with cherries

SERVES 2

8 tbsp wheat grains
200 g (6½ oz) sour cherries
   (from the jar)
2 tsp dextrose
200 g (6½ oz) cream
PREPARATION: about 10 mins
CHILLING: about 12 hrs

1. Coarsely crush or "kibble" the wheat in a cereal mill. Stir in 120 ml (4 fl oz/½ cup) cold water, cover and chill for about 12 hours or overnight in the refrigerator.

2. Drain the sour cherries, then fold them into the cereal. Sweeten to taste with dextrose.

3. Beat the cream until stiff, then gently fold into the cherry muesli. Divide the wheat muesli between two breakfast bowls and serve.

TIP

This muesli will fill you up for a long time. If you like a sharpish flavour, replace the water with 120 ml (4 fl oz/½ cup) lemon juice. During the test phase you could also add other (tolerated) fruits in the muesli. At the start of the test phase prepare your muesli with cream. Its higher fat content will make the fructose easier to digest. If you tolerate it well, you can then change over to yoghurt (3.5% fat).

NUTRITIONAL VALUES PER PORTION:
500 Cal • 8 g protein • 33 g fat • 43 g carbohydrate

Delicious White Bread

**MAKES 16 SLICES
(1 LOAF TIN, 30 CM/12 IN)**

650 g (1 lb 4 oz) wholemeal
   wheat flour
2 tsp salt
1 cube fresh yeast (42 g/1½ oz)
   or 1 tbsp dried yeast
butter, for greasing
PREPARATION: about 15 mins
BAKING: about 50 mins

1. Preheat the oven to 200°C/180°C fan-forced (middle shelf). Combine the flour and the salt. Crumble the fresh yeast or sprinkle the dried yeast on top.

2. Using the kneading hook of a hand-held blender, slowly stir in 500 ml (16 fl oz/2 cups) lukewarm water. Continue kneading until you have a firm dough.

3. Grease the loaf tin, then place the dough into the tin. Bake the bread in the oven for about 50 minutes until golden.

TIP

If you prefer a grainy bread, simply knead an additional 100 g (3⅓ oz) sunflower, sesame, poppy seeds or linseed into the dough. If you add seeds use 600 ml (20 fl oz/2½ cups) water.

NUTRITIONAL VALUES PER PORTION:
135 Cal • 5 g protein • 1 g fat • 27 g carbohydrate

Yoghurt Bread

MAKES 20 SLICES (1 LOAF)

butter, for greasing
flour, for dusting
300 g (10 oz) wholemeal
   wheat flour
300 g (10 oz) plain flour
2 tsp baking powder
3 tbsp dextrose
1 tsp salt
1 egg
425 g (14 oz) yoghurt
PREPARATION: about 15 mins
BAKING: about 40 mins

1. Preheat the oven to 200°C/180°C fan-forced (middle shelf). Grease and dust a baking tray. Combine the two flours, the baking powder, the dextrose and the salt. Whisk together the egg and the yoghurt.

2. Stir the flour mixture into the yoghurt mixture using the kneading hook of a hand-held blender. Dust the work surface with flour. Knead the mixture until you have a smooth dough.

3. Shape the dough into a round loaf and place it on the baking tray. Cut a cross into the top.

4. Bake the bread in the oven for about 40 minutes until golden. Take out and place on a wire rack to cool completely.

SPEEDY

This delicious bread uses only baking powder to make the dough rise, and so it can be prepared quickly.

NUTRITIONAL VALUES PER PORTION:
125 Cal • 4 g protein • 1 g fat • 24 g carbohydrate

Berry Jam

MAKES 3 JARS OF 400 G/13 OZ

1 kg (2 lb 4 oz) mixed berries
    (fresh or frozen)
500 g (1 lb) dextrose
1 pack gelling agent
2 tsp liquid sweetener

PREPARATION: about 20 mins

1. Carefully wash, pat dry and hull the berries or allow the frozen fruit to thaw.

2. Using a hand-held blender, finely purée the berries, then press the fruit purée through a fine sieve into the saucepan.

3. Combine the dextrose with the gelling agent. Stir into the berry purée together with the liquid sweetener.

4. Bring the berry and sugar mixture to the boil. Cook for 3 minutes, stirring constantly. Pour into sterilised screw-top jars while still hot and seal immediately.

TIP

The jam will keep for about 3 months in a sealed jar. Once opened however you should use the contents within about 2 weeks.

NUTRITIONAL VALUES PER PORTION:

30 Cal • 0 g protein • < 1 g fat • 7 g carbohydrate

Apricot Spread

MAKES 2 JARS OF 400 G/13 OZ

200 g (6½ oz) dried apricots
  (unsulphurised)
250 g (8 oz) dextrose
PREPARATION: about 60 mins
SOAKING: about 12 hrs

1. Wash the apricots. Pour over 500 ml (16 fl oz/2 cups) water, cover and leave to soak for about 12 hours or overnight.

2. Using a food processor or a hand-held blender, roughly purée the fruits together with the soaking water.

3. Stir the dextrose into the apricot purée in a saucepan and bring to the boil. Cook uncovered over low heat for 40 minutes, stirring occasionally, until you have a thick spread.

4. Pour the spread into sterilised screw-top jars while hot and seal immediately. Will keep for 3 months while sealed; once opened use within 2 weeks.

TIP

This spread is particularly tasty on white bread (see page 28) with a little cream cheese. The Apricot Spread also makes a tasty filling, for example in an Orange and Chocolate Cake (see page 118).

NUTRITIONAL VALUES PER PORTION:
30 Cal • 0 g protein • < 1 g fat • 7 g carbohydrate

Vanilla Cherry Cream

MAKES 2 JARS OF 450 G/15 OZ

1 jar sour cherries (680 g/
  1 lb 5 oz drained weight)
400 g (13 oz) dextrose
2 packets instant vanilla custard
  powder (for 500 ml/16 fl oz/
  2 cups milk)
PREPARATION: about 20 mins

1. Set aside 100 ml (3 fl oz/½ cup) cherry juice. Using a food processor or a hand-held blender, finely purée the cherries with the remaining juice.

2. In a saucepan bring the cherry purée and the dextrose to the boil. Meanwhile, whisk the custard powder into the reserved cherry juice.

3. Stir the custard mixture into the hot cherry purée. Cook for 1 minute, stirring constantly. Pour into sterilised screw-top jars while hot and seal immediately. Keeps for 1 month when sealed; once opened use within 2 weeks.

TIP

A couple of spoons of Vanilla Cherry Cream will quickly turn your cream cheese or yoghurt into a delicious fruity dessert.

NUTRITIONAL VALUES PER PORTION:
35 Cal • 0 g protein • < 1 g fat • 9 g carbohydrate

Chocolate Butter

MAKES 1 JAR OF 300 G/10 OZ

250 g (8 oz) soft butter

6 tbsp dextrose

3 tbsp cocoa powder

PREPARATION: about 10 mins

1. Using a hand-held blender, whisk the butter with the dextrose and the cocoa until you have a smooth cream.

2. Place the chocolate butter into a screw-top jar and seal it. It will keep at room temperature for about 14 days.

TIP

Everyone will love this spread, especially children will want nothing else for breakfast!

NUTRITIONAL VALUES PER PORTION:

155 Cal • 1 g protein • 14 g fat • 6 g carbohydrate

Nut & Nougat Cream

SERVES 2

5 tbsp dextrose

3 tbsp ground hazelnuts

1 tbsp cocoa powder

3 tbsp sour cream

PREPARATION: about 10 mins

1. Combine the dextrose with the nuts and the cocoa.

2. Stir in the sour cream to make a smooth mixture.

3. Divide the cream mixture between two bowls and serve.

TIP

It's unlikely but just in case you have some of the cream mixture left over, simply keep in a small container in the fridge. The cream will stay fresh for a few days. The Nut & Nougat Cream also tastes delicious with ground almonds.

NUTRITIONAL VALUES PER PORTION:

265 Cal • 3 g protein • 11 g fat • 40 g carbohydrate

Sweet Almond Spread

SERVES 2

100 g (3⅓ oz) cream cheese
50 g (1⅔ oz) ground almonds
2 tbsp dextrose
1–2 drops bitter almond extract

PREPARATION: about 10 mins

1. Using a fork, thoroughly combine the cream cheese with the almonds, the dextrose and the bitter almond extract.

2. Divide the spread between two small bowls and serve. Any leftovers will keep for about 1 week if the spread is stored in a sealed container in the fridge.

VARIATION

You have no almonds in the cupboard? Make the spread with ground roasted walnuts or cashew nuts and a pinch of cinnamon instead.

NUTRITIONAL VALUES PER PORTION:
350 Cal • 8 g protein • 28 g fat • 17 g carbohydrate

Banana & Coconut Cream

SERVES 2

1 ripe banana
1 tsp cocoa powder
2 tbsp sour cream
3 tbsp dextrose
2 tbsp grated coconut

PREPARATION: about 10 mins

1. Peel the banana and mash it well with a fork.

2. Stir the cocoa, sour cream and dextrose into the purée, then fold in the grated coconut.

3. Divide the cream between two small bowls and serve. Keep any leftovers in a tightly sealed container and store in the fridge. Use the cream within 1 week.

NUTRITIONAL VALUES PER PORTION:
235 Cal • 2 g protein • 10 g fat • 35 g carbohydrate

Cheesy Butter

SERVES 2–3

25 g (¾ oz) Parmesan
25 g (¾ oz) Swiss cheese
15 g (½ oz) mild Camembert
60 g (2 oz) soft butter
1 tbsp milk (if needed)
white pepper
sweet paprika
ground caraway seeds

PREPARATION: about 15 mins
CHILLING: about 2 hrs

1. Finely grate the Parmesan and the Swiss cheese. Chop the Camembert into small dice.

2. Using a hand-held blender, whisk the different cheese with the butter until creamy. If the mixture seems too dry, simply add a little milk.

3. Season the cheese mixture with pepper, paprika and ground caraway seeds to taste. Divide into small portions and chill for about 2 hours before using.

NUTRITIONAL VALUES PER PORTION:
230 Cal • 7 g protein • 22 g fat • 1 g carbohydrate

Red Basil Butter

SERVES 2–3

¼ bunch basil
60 g (2 oz) soft butter
1 tbsp tomato paste
½ spring onion
pepper
sweet paprika

PREPARATION: about 15 mins
CHILLING: about 2 hrs

1. Wash and pat dry the basil. Pull off the leaves and roughly chop them.

2. Mash the butter with a fork, then stir in the basil and the tomato paste.

3. Peel and finely chop the spring onion, then fold it into the basil butter.

4. Season the butter to taste with pepper and paprika. Divide into small portions and chill for about 2 hours before using.

NUTRITIONAL VALUES PER PORTION:
155 Cal • 0 g protein • 17 g fat • 1 g carbohydrate

Salmon Butter

SERVES 2–3

50 g (1²/₃ oz) soft butter

1–2 tsp dill

½ spring onion

30 g (1 oz) salmon

salt, pepper

1 pinch grated zest of an
  organic lemon

PREPARATION: about 10 mins

CHILLING: about 2 hrs

1. Beat the butter with the dill until foamy.

2. Peel and finely chop the spring onion, then stir into the dill and butter mixture.

3. Using a fork, flake the salmon, then fold the fish into the creamy butter mixture.

4. Season the butter with salt, pepper and lemon zest to taste. Divide the butter into small portions and chill for about 2 hours before using.

NUTRITIONAL VALUES PER PORTION:

155 Cal • 3 g protein • 16 g fat • 0 g carbohydrate

Parmesan & Egg Spread

SERVES 2–3

2 eggs

90 g (3 oz) Parmesan

50 g (1²/₃ oz) soft butter

PREPARATION: about 15 mins

CHILLING: about 2 hrs

1. Boil the eggs for 10 minutes until hard. Refresh under cold water, shell and chop the eggs. Finely grate the Parmesan.

2. Beat the butter until foamy, then stir in the chopped egg and the cheese. Divide into serving portions and chill for about 2 hours before serving.

STORE CUPBOARD

This savoury spread can easily be made ahead of time. Store in a tightly sealed container and chill in the fridge for up to 5 days.

NUTRITIONAL VALUES PER PORTION:

290 Cal • 16 g protein • 25 g fat • 0 g carbohydrate

Seaside Breakfast

SERVES 2

2 tsp white vinegar

250 g (8 oz) fish fillet (e.g. salmon)

salt

1½ gherkins (from the jar)

2 boiled potatoes (from the
  day before)

2 radishes

3 sprigs fresh dill

75 g (2¾ oz) yoghurt

25 g (¾ oz) cream cheese

1 tsp tomato paste

1-2 tbsp cream

½ tsp grated horseradish (jar)

sweet paprika, salt, pepper, dextrose

a few lettuce leaves

PREPARATION: about 35 mins

1. Stir the vinegar into 4 teaspoons water. Wash the fish under cold water, then pat dry. Drizzle the fish with the vinegar water, sprinkle with salt and set aside for 10 minutes.

2. In a saucepan, bring the fish and its marinade to the boil over medium heat. Turn off the heat, cover the saucepan and leave to infuse for 15 minutes.

3. Drain the gherkins and finely chop them. Cut the potatoes into 1 cm (½ in) pieces. Wash, trim, halve and slice the radishes. Wash the dill, then shake it dry. Finely chop 1 sprig.

4. Stir together the yoghurt with the cream cheese, tomato paste, cream and horseradish. Season to taste with the chopped dill, paprika, salt, pepper and dextrose.

5. Fold the gherkins, potatoes and radishes into the yoghurt and cream mixture. Chop the fish into bite-sized pieces and gently fold in.

6. Wash, then spin-dry the lettuce and divide between two serving bowls. Pile the fish mixture on top and garnish each bowl with a sprig of dill.

NUTRITIONAL VALUES PER PORTION:
230 Cal • 28 g protein • 6 g fat • 16 g carbohydrate

Breakfast Bake

SERVES 2

2 slices white bread

1 slice ham

2 eggs

60 ml (2 fl oz/¼ cup) milk

60 g (2 oz) cream

salt, pepper

1 tbsp grated cheese
  (e.g. Cheddar)

butter, for greasing

PREPARATION: about 25 mins

CHILLING: about 12 hrs

BAKING: about 35 mins

1. Preheat the oven to 180°C/160°C fan-forced (middle shelf). Cut the bread and the ham into small pieces.

2. Whisk the eggs together with the milk and cream. Season to taste with salt and pepper. Stir in the cheese, bread and ham.

3. Grease a baking dish and pour in the egg mixture. Smooth over the surface. Cover and chill for about 12 hours or overnight.

4. Bake in the oven for about 35 minutes until golden.

TIP

This bake can easily be prepared ahead of time. For a change stir finely chopped vegetables into the egg mixture, such as broccoli, tomatoes or carrots.

NUTRITIONAL VALUES PER PORTION:

280 Cal • 13 g protein • 18 g fat • 17 g carbohydrate

Eggs and Toast with spinach

SERVES 2

½ small onion

3 tsp butter

250 g (8 oz) frozen spinach

salt, pepper, nutmeg

2 eggs

2 tbsp mineral water

1 tbsp chopped garlic

1 tbsp chopped chives

2 tbsp grated cheese

2 slices wholemeal wheat bread

2 cherry tomatoes

PREPARATION: about 30 mins

1. Peel and finely chop the onion. In a saucepan, heat 1 teaspoon butter and fry the chopped onion until translucent. Add the spinach and defrost over low heat, stirring occasionally. Season the mixture to taste with salt, pepper and nutmeg.

2. Using a hand-held blender, whisk the eggs and the mineral water until foaming. Stir in the garlic, chives and cheese. Season to taste with salt and pepper.

3. Heat 1 teaspoon butter in a frying pan. Pour in the egg mixture and cook over low heat until it sets. Gently stir and continue frying the scrambled egg, until golden and firm.

4. Toast the bread. Spread the slices with the remaining butter and cover with the spinach. Spread the scrambled egg on top.

5. Wash and thinly slice the tomatoes. Serve them arranged on top of the eggs.

NUTRITIONAL VALUES PER PORTION:

245 Cal • 13 g protein • 14 g fat • 18 g carbohydrate

Grapefruit Drink with cherry ice

MAKES 2 GLASSES

50 ml (2 fl oz/¼ cup) cherry nectar

½ grapefruit

100 ml (3 fl oz/½ cup) orange juice

1 tbsp dextrose

150 ml (5 fl oz/¾ cup) diet
   orange cordial

PREPARATION: about 10 mins

FREEZING: about 2 hrs

1. Fill the cherry nectar into an ice-cube mould and place in the freezer for about 2 hours to make red cherry ice cubes.

2. Squeeze the grapefruit. Combine the juice with the orange juice and the dextrose. Stir in the orangeade.

3. Divide the cherry ice cubes between two tall glasses. Pour the juice mixture on top and serve immediately.

TIP

Once the cherry-red ice cubes are frozen, this drink is quickly assembled. However, don't drink this until you are in the test phase.

NUTRITIONAL VALUES PER PORTION:

85 Cal • 1 g protein • < 1 g fat • 19 g carbohydrate

Blueberry Smoothie

MAKES 2 GLASSES

75 g (2¾ oz) blueberries
   (fresh or frozen)

50 g (1⅔ oz) dextrose

¼ tsp liquid sweetener

300 g (10 oz) creamy natural yoghurt

100 ml (3 fl oz/½ cup) milk

2 straws

PREPARATION: about 10 mins

1. Gently wash, then pat dry the berries. Leave frozen fruits to defrost. With a food processor or a hand-held blender, finely purée the berries together with the dextrose and the sweetener.

2. Stir together the yoghurt and the milk and pour into two tall glasses. Top the yoghurt milk with the berry purée. Put a straw into each glass and stir to create berry swirls.

TIP

You can make this tasty yoghurt drink with any other berries that you can tolerate.

NUTRITIONAL VALUES PER PORTION:

235 Cal • 7 g protein • 7 g fat • 36 g carbohydrate

Vanilla Buttermilk with wheat bran

MAKES 2 GLASSES

3 tbsp dextrose

2-3 drops vanilla essence

400 ml (14 fl oz/1¾ cups) buttermilk

2 tsp wheat bran (alternatively ground
   hazelnuts or almonds)

PREPARATION: about 10 mins

1. Whisk the dextrose and the vanilla into the buttermilk.

2. Pour the vanilla milk into two tall glasses and sprinkle each glass with
   1 teaspoon wheat bran. Serve immediately.

VARIATION

You'd prefer a hot chocolate drink? Heat 400 ml (14 fl oz/1¾ cups) milk.
Combine 1 teaspoon cocoa and 2 tablespoons dextrose, then stir in. If you like,
flavour your cocoa with a pinch of cinnamon or a spoonful of Almond Spread.

NUTRITIONAL VALUES PER PORTION:

165 Cal • 7 g protein • 1 g fat • 31 g carbohydrate

Peach & Kiwi Fruit Punch

MAKES 2 GLASSES

2 ripe peaches (alternatively
   nectarines, apricots or bananas)

1 kiwi fruit

150 ml (5 fl oz/¾ cup) orange juice

3 tsp lemon juice

1 tsp dextrose

150 ml (5 fl oz/¾ cup) mineral water

PREPARATION: about 15 mins

1. Briefly plunge the peaches into boiling water, rinse, then peel. Halve
   the fruits and remove the kernels. Purée 2 halves in a food processor or
   using a hand-held blender; chop the rest.

2. Peel and halve the kiwi fruit; cut into slices. Put 2 slices with 2 peach
   pieces on a skewer.

3. Whisk together the orange juice, lemon juice, dextrose and peach
   purée. Stir in the fruits and the mineral water.

4. Place some ice cubes (if using) into two tall glasses. Top with the punch,
   garnish with the fruit skewer and serve.

NUTRITIONAL VALUES PER PORTION:

100 Cal • 2 g protein • < 1 g fat • 22 g carbohydrate

Cucumber & Tomato Salad

SERVES 2

2 tsp white wine vinegar

¼ tsp mustard

salt, pepper

3 tsp rapeseed oil

½ cucumber

150 g (5 oz) tomatoes

¼ bunch chives

PREPARATION: about 20 mins

1. Whisk together the vinegar with the mustard, salt, pepper and oil.

2. Trim and thinly peel the cucumber, then halve it lengthways. Thinly slice the halves. Wash the tomatoes and remove the ends. Cut the tomatoes into eighths and combine with the cucumber.

3. Wash and shake dry the chives, then snip or chop and sprinkle over the salad.

4. Drizzle the dressing over the salad and gently stir. Generously season the salad, divide into portions and serve.

TIP

If the salad is not meant to be eaten straightaway, scrape out the cucumber seeds with a teaspoon. This stops it absorbing too much water and keeps it tasty.

NUTRITIONAL VALUES PER PORTION:

60 Cal • 1 g protein • 5 g fat • 3 g carbohydrate

Sweetcorn Salad with tuna and tomato

SERVES 2

150 g (5 oz) sweetcorn (tinned)

75 g (2¾ oz) tuna in spring water (tinned)

250 g (8 oz) tomatoes

8-10 fresh basil leaves

2 tsp olive oil

1 tsp lemon juice concentrate (alternatively lemon juice)

salt, pepper

PREPARATION: about 10 mins

1. Drain the tinned sweetcorn and the tuna.

2. Wash the tomatoes and remove the ends. Cut the tomatoes into dice. Combine with the sweetcorn and the tuna.

3. Wash, then pat dry the basil leaves. Tear into small pieces and sprinkle over the salad.

4. Whisk together the oil with the lemon juice concentrate and a little salt and pepper. Drizzle the dressing over the salad and gently stir in.

TIP

Lemon juice concentrate does not contain any fructose because it is an artificial product. If only very small quantities are required, you can use fresh lemon juice instead.

NUTRITIONAL VALUES PER PORTION:

320 Cal • 15 g protein • 7 g fat • 51 g carbohydrate

Feta & Pasta Salad

SERVES 2

250 g (8 oz) fusilli (spiral pasta)

salt

½ cucumber

½ bunch spring onions

2 tomatoes

150 g (5 oz) feta

100 g (3⅓ oz) natural yoghurt
   (3.5% fat)

500 g (1 lb) tomato purée

1 garlic clove, peeled and crushed

pepper, paprika

PREPARATION: about 30 mins
MARINATING: about 30 mins

1. Cook the pasta in boiling salted water as per packet instructions until al dente (firm to the bite). Drain and leave to cool.

2. Trim and thinly peel the cucumber, then halve it lengthways. Scrape out the seeds and slice the halves. Wash and trim the spring onions, then cut them into thin rings. Wash the tomatoes and remove the stem ends. Chop the tomatoes and the feta.

3. Whisk together the yoghurt and the tomato purée. Stir in the garlic. Season the dressing to taste with salt, pepper and paprika.

4. Fold the pasta, vegetables and cheese into the dressing. Leave to marinate for about 30 minutes. Check the seasoning and serve.

LUNCHTIME SNACK

This filling salad is perfect for your lunch. It is particularly good when you are changing your diet as this is a time when you should do without ready-made meals where the fructose contents may not be clear.

NUTRITIONAL VALUES PER PORTION:

735 Cal • 35 g protein • 18 g fat • 107 g carbohydrate

Fresh Cheese Salad

SERVES 2

100 g (3⅓ oz) Edam cheese

50 g (1⅔ oz) ham

1 gherkin (from the jar)

¼ cucumber

½ yellow capsicum (pepper)

½ marinated red capsicum

75 g (2¾ oz) low-fat yoghurt (0.1% fat)

2 tsp sour cream

½ tsp horseradish cream (from the jar)

½ bunch dill

¼ tsp glucose

1 tsp lemon juice concentrate
   (alternatively lemon juice)

salt, pepper

PREPARATION: about 30 mins

1. Cut the Edam cheese into 1 cm (½ in) pieces. Cut the ham into thin strips.

2. Drain the gherkin. Thinly peel the cucumber. Wash and trim the capsicum. Chop the gherkin, cucumber, capsicum and marinated capsicum into small dice.

3. Combine the cheese, ham strips and vegetables. Fold in the yoghurt, sour cream and horseradish.

4. Wash and shake dry the dill, then snip into thin strips using kitchen scissors and sprinkle over the salad.

5. Season the salad with the glucose, lemon juice concentrate, salt and pepper. Leave to marinate for another 10 minutes. Check the seasoning again and divide between bowls to serve.

TIP

This salad is especially well tolerated during the abstention phase. It can easily be made ahead of time and, with a bread roll, it is an ideal snack on the go.

NUTRITIONAL VALUES PER PORTION:

205 Cal • 22 g protein • 10 g fat • 7 g carbohydrate

Asian Chicken Salad

SERVES 2

200 g (6½ oz) chicken breast fillet

½ leek

2 tsp oil

1 small garlic clove, peeled
   and crushed

1 piece fresh ginger
   (about 1 cm/½ in)

3 tsp mayonnaise

150 g (5 oz) natural yoghurt
   (3.5% fat)

3 tsp orange juice

1 tsp lemon juice (if tolerated)

salt, curry powder

PREPARATION: about 30 mins

1. Wash and pat dry the meat, then cut into thin strips.

2. Trim the leek, halve it lengthways and throughly wash it. Cut the halves into very fine strips.

3. Heat the oil in a frying pan and fry the meat and leek strips.

4. Peel and finely grate the ginger and add to the pan with the garlic. Continue frying until the meat and the leek are lightly browned. Remove and leave to cool.

5. Whisk together the mayonnaise and the yoghurt, orange juice and lemon juice. Drizzle the dressing over the salad, then gently stir to combine. Season generously with salt and curry powder.

TIP

Leek will not give you any digestive problems if it has been briefly fried.

NUTRITIONAL VALUES PER PORTION:
245 Cal • 26 g protein • 13 g fat • 6 g carbohydrate

Nutty Fennel & Kiwi Fruit Salad

SERVES 2

1 fennel bulb

8 walnut kernels

150 g (5 oz) natural yoghurt
   (3.5% fat)

100 g (3⅓ oz) sour cream

1 tbsp lemon juice (if tolerated)

2 tsp glucose

salt, pepper

1 kiwi fruit

PREPARATION: about 20 mins

1. Wash, then halve the fennel. Remove the stem and the hard core. Finely dice the halves. Finely chop the walnut kernels.

2. Whisk together the yoghurt and the sour cream, lemon juice, glucose, salt and pepper. Fold in the fennel and the walnuts.

3. Peel and dice the kiwi fruit. Stir the dice into the salad and serve immediately.

TIP

Only stir the kiwi fruit into the salad just before you are ready to serve. The kiwi fruit will quickly give the salad a bitter flavour.

NUTRITIONAL VALUES PER PORTION:
210 Cal • 8 g protein • 14 g fat • 13 g carbohydrate

Carrot Salad with toasted cashew nuts

SERVES 2

250 g (8 oz) carrots

1 small garlic clove, peeled
and crushed

125 g (4 oz) natural yoghurt
(3.5% fat)

1 piece fresh ginger
(about 2 cm/½ in)

salt, curry powder

1 tsp glucose

1 tsp lemon juice (if tolerated)

50 g (1²/₃ oz) cashew kernels

PREPARATION: about 30 mins

1. Trim and thinly peel, then finely grate the carrots. Pile the carrot gratings into two glasses.

2. Add the crushed garlic to the yoghurt. Peel the ginger and finely grate it with a fine kitchen grater. Add to the yoghurt. Stir to combine.

3. Generously season the yoghurt with salt, curry powder, glucose and lemon juice. Drizzle the dressing over the carrots, but don't stir in.

4. In a non-stick frying pan, dry-roast the cashew kernels over medium heat without adding any fat. Stir constantly until golden. Roughly chop the nuts and sprinkle over the salad.

TIP

If you like, you could stir 1 pinch turmeric into the dressing. This gives it an intense yellow colour – making the salad attractive to look at as well as tasty. Gentle dry-roasting brings out the delicate aroma of the cashews particularly well. But watch out: if the heat is too strong, roasting quickly becomes too fierce and the delicate aroma will be destroyed.

NUTRITIONAL VALUES PER PORTION:
225 Cal • 8 g protein • 13 g fat • 19 g carbohydrate

Thousand Island Dressing

SERVES 2

125 g (4 oz) mayonnaise

60 g (2 oz) low-fat cream cheese

1 tbsp sour cream

50 g (1²/₃ oz) tomato purée (tinned)

1 gherkin (from the jar)

salt, pepper

sweet paprika

glucose

PREPARATION: about 10 mins

1. Whisk together the mayonnaise with the cream cheese and the sour cream. Stir in the tomato purée.

2. Drain the gherkin and chop into very small dice. Stir into the dressing.

3. Season the dressing to taste with salt, pepper, paprika and glucose.

ALLROUNDER

This dressing goes well with leafy salads and raw vegetables, but it is also tasty with steamed vegetables, chicken salad or potatoes.

NUTRITIONAL VALUES PER PORTION:

500 Cal • 5 g protein • 51 g fat • 4 g carbohydrate

Yoghurt Salad Cream

SERVES 2

100 g (3¹/₃ oz) cucumber ✽

1 small onion (25 g/¾ oz)

½ bunch chervil or parsley

150 g (5 oz) low-fat natural yoghurt
(0.1% fat)

50 g (1²/₃ oz) creamy yoghurt
(10% fat)

1 pinch glucose

salt, white pepper

PREPARATION: about 10 mins

1. Thinly peel the cucumber, halve it lengthways and scrape out the seeds. Cut the halves into thin sticks.

2. Peel the onion. Wash and shake dry the chervil. Finely chop both.

3. Whisk together the natural and the creamy yoghurt. Season with glucose, salt and pepper. Fold in the cucumber sticks, onion and chervil. Leave the salad cream to marinate for a while. Check the seasoning again before serving.

VERSATILE

This salad cream goes particularly well with potato dishes and with roasted or fried meat.

NUTRITIONAL VALUES PER PORTION:
50 Cal • 2 g protein • 3 g fat • 4 g carbohydrate

Peanut & Sesame Sauce

SERVES 2

1 egg

50 g (1²/₃ oz) unsalted peanut kernels

2 tsp sesame seeds

225 g (7½ oz) creamy yoghurt
(10% fat)

1 tsp Dijon mustard

salt, pepper

glucose

PREPARATION: about 20 mins

1. Hard-boil the egg for about 10 minutes. Rinse under cold water, shell the egg and cut it into small dice.

2. In a non-stick frying pan, dry-roast the peanuts and sesame seeds without fat until golden. Finely chop both in a blender.

3. Whisk together the yoghurt and the mustard. Stir in the egg and the nut mixture. Season with salt, pepper and glucose.

TIP

This nutty sauce is a tasty accompaniment for grilled meat and poultry.

CAUTION: TRAP

Ready-made BBQ sauces and dressings often contain large amounts of sugar. It's an easy trap to avoid. Just collect any „tasty", „easy to prepare" sauce and dip recipes that you come across so you have them on hand when required.

NUTRITIONAL VALUES PER PORTION:
335 Cal • 14 g protein • 28 g fat • 7 g carbohydrate

Cream of Pumpkin Soup

SERVES 2–3

½ Japanese pumpkin
  (350 g/11½ oz)
1 carrot (100 g/3⅓ oz)
175 g (5⅔ oz) potatoes
500 ml (16 fl oz/2 cups)
  vegetable stock
100 g (3⅓ oz) cream
1 tsp lemon juice (if tolerated)
salt, pepper, curry powder
2 tsp pumpkin seeds
PREPARATION: about 40 mins

1. Wash, then quarter the pumpkin and scrape out the seeds. Cut the quarter into pieces of about 2 cm (¾ in).

2. Trim and thinly peel the carrot, then cut into dice. Peel, then wash and dice the potatoes. In a saucepan, bring the stock to the boil with the pumpkin, carrot and potato. Cook for 10 minutes, until the pumpkin skin is soft.

3. Using the mixer or a hand-held blender, purée the soup until creamy. Stir in the cream and the lemon juice. Season the soup with salt, pepper and curry powder.

4. Finely chop the pumpkin seeds. Divide the soup between bowls and sprinkle with the pumpkin seeds.

SKIN ON

Do leave the pumpkin skin on when cooking – it adds flavour. If you are already in the test phase, you can season your soup additionally with 1 garlic clove as well as 1 pinch freshly grated ginger. It will give it that certain something.

NUTRITIONAL VALUES PER PORTION:
190 Cal • 4 g protein • 12 g fat • 16 g carbohydrate

Potato Soup with salmon

SERVES 2

1 small onion
½ bunch spring onions
175 g (5⅔ oz) potatoes
1 tsp margarine
300 ml (10 fl oz/1¼ cups) vegetable
  stock
125 g (4 oz) smoked salmon
salt, pepper
1 dash lemon juice (if tolerated)
50 g (1⅔ oz) sour cream
PREPARATION: about 35 mins

1. Peel and finely chop the onion. Wash and trim the spring onions, then chop into fine rings including the green parts. Wash and peel the potatoes, then grate into thin sticks.

2. In a saucepan heat the margarine and fry the onion until translucent. Sprinkle in the grated potato and fry, stirring constantly. Stir in the spring onion rings.

3. Pour in the stock. Bring to the boil and leave to simmer over low heat for 10 minutes.

4. Cut the salmon into thin strips and briefly warm the strips in the soup. Season the soup with salt, pepper and lemon juice. Fold in the sour cream and briefly warm through.

TIP

This soup is full of nutrients. It's generally well tolerated, especially when you are in the process of changing your diet and quickly calms down an 'unruly' stomach.

NUTRITIONAL VALUES PER PIECE:
330 Cal • 22 g protein • 21 g fat • 14 g carbohydrate

Curried Banana Soup

SERVES 2–3

1 spring onion

1 small garlic clove

1½ bananas

1 level tbsp margarine

2 tsp curry powder

1 heaped tbsp flour

500 ml (16 fl oz/2 cups)
   chicken stock

salt, white pepper

75 g (2¾ oz) sour cream

PREPARATION: about 20 mins

1. Peel and finely chop the spring onion and the garlic clove. Peel the whole banana and mash with a fork.

2. Heat the margarine in a saucepan and fry the spring onion and garlic until translucent. Sprinkle in the curry powder and continue frying until browned. Stir in the mashed banana and sprinkle the flour on top; fry for 2 minutes until browned. Pour in the stock and briefly bring to the boil.

3. Season the soup to taste with salt, pepper and curry powder. Using a mixer or a hand-held blender, purée the mixture until creamy. Fold in the sour cream.

4. Peel the half banana and roughly mash it with a fork, then stir into the soup. Briefly warm through again.

TIP

This savoury soup has a pleasantly tropical flavour, combining fruit and Indian spices. It is a warming winter snack but it can also be enjoyed well chilled on a hot summer's day.

NUTRITIONAL VALUES PER PORTION:
195 Cal • 13 g protein • 9 g fat • 15 g carbohydrate

Vegetable Soup

SERVES 2

½ red capsicum (pepper,
   75 g/2¾ oz)

25 g (¾ oz) celeriac

1 tbsp oil

200 g (6½ oz) chopped
   tomatoes (tinned)

1 tbsp tomato paste

250 ml (8 fl oz/1 cup) vegetable stock

1 small garlic clove, peeled
   and crushed

1 tsp balsamic vinegar

1 tsp glucose

5 tbsp cream

salt, pepper

½ bunch basil

PREPARATION: about 20 mins

1. Wash and trim the capsicum. Thinly peel the celeriac. Chop both into small dice.

2. Heat the oil in a saucepan and fry the vegetables for about 5 minutes, stirring constantly. Stir in the chopped tomatoes, tomato paste and vegetable stock. Quickly bring to the boil.

3. Add the crushed garlic to the soup. Stir in the vinegar, glucose and cream. Season the soup with salt and pepper.

4. Wash and pat dry the basil, then finely chop the leaves. Divide the soup between two soup bowls and sprinkle with the chopped basil leaves.

NUTRITIONAL VALUES PER PIECE:
175 Cal • 3 g protein • 14 g fat • 9 g carbohydrate

Pancake Wraps with ham and olives

SERVES 2–3
FOR THE BATTER
150 ml (5 fl oz/¾ cup) milk
200 g (6½ oz) plain flour
2 eggs
1 tsp salt
oil, for frying
FOR THE HAM FILLING
½ red capsicum (pepper,
   75 g/2¾ oz)
100 g (3⅓ oz) ham
150 g (5 oz) herbed cream cheese
2–3 tbsp milk (if needed)
salt, pepper, paprika
FOR THE OLIVE FILLING
50 g (1²/₃ oz) green olives
   (from the jar)
50 g (1²/₃ oz) sundried tomatoes in
   oil (from the jar)
150 g (5 oz) cream cheese
1 small garlic clove, peeled
   and crushed
PREPARATION: about 60 mins

1. To make the batter, stir a little milk into the flour. Gradually add the remaining milk plus 200 ml (7 fl oz/¾ cup) water, until you have a smooth batter. Whisk in the eggs and salt.

2. Heat the oil in a non-stick frying pan. Pour in a ladle of the batter and distribute evenly in the pan. Cook the pancake over medium heat for 1–2 minutes, turn it over and briefly cook the other side. Transfer the cooked pancake to a plate and leave to cool. Cook another 5 thin pancakes in the same way.

3. To make the ham filling, wash and trim the capsicum. Cut the capsicum and the ham into small dice. Combine with the cream cheese, stirring in a little milk if the mixture is too dry. Season with salt, pepper and paprika.

4. To make the olive filling, drain the olives and tomatoes, then pat dry with kitchen paper. Chop both into small pieces and stir into the cream cheese. Add the crushed garlic to the mixture.

5. Spread three pancakes with ham filling and three with olive filling, then roll up. Cut the rolls in half diagonally, transfer to plates and serve cold.

TIP
You can vary the fillings as you desire. These pancake wraps are also delicious with a sweet Nut & Nougat Cream (see page 32). Children usually love these pancakes – they are best eaten with your hands.

VARIATION
To make Tuna Wraps, drain 1 tin tuna in water (200 g/6½ oz drained weight). Peel and finely chop 1 small onion. Stir together the fish with 3 tablespoons mayonnaise and 1 tablespoon lemon juice concentrate. Season generously with salt and pepper. Fill the pancakes as per the recipe.

NUTRITIONAL VALUES PER PORTION:
720 Cal • 28 g protein • 40 g fat • 62 g carbohydrate

Ham & Olive balls

MAKES 20 PIECES

1 garlic clove

170 g (5½ oz) Cheddar cheese

250 g (8 oz) plain flour

175 g (5²/₃ oz) margarine

salt, white pepper

100 g (3¹/₃ oz) prosciutto

flour, for dusting

100 g (3¹/₃ oz) olives

5 tbsp cream (alternatively
  unsweetened condensed milk)

50 g (1²/₃ oz) hulled sesame seeds

PREPARATION: about 15 mins

BAKING: about 25 mins

1. Peel the garlic. Finely chop the garlic and the cheese. Knead the flour and margarine together until you have a smooth dough. Knead in the cheese, garlic, salt and pepper.

2. Preheat the oven to 180°C/160°C fan-forced (middle shelf). Line a baking tray with baking paper. Chop the prosciutto into small pieces.

3. On a floured surface, roll out the dough as a roll, about 3 cm (1¼ in) thick. Cut the roll into 20 slices. Make a hollow in each slice and fill this with the chopped prosciutto and olives. Fold together and shape as balls.

4. Turn the balls first in the cream, then in the sesame seeds and place them on the baking tray. Bake the balls for about 25 minutes until golden.

TIP

These crispy balls are a welcome snack, especially during the abstention phase when they will bridge the long periods between meals. For a change you can also fill them with finely diced turkey breast, ham or spicy chorizo sausage.

NUTRITIONAL VALUES PER PORTION:

185 Cal • 5 g protein • 14 g fat • 9 g carbohydrate

Tomato Dip

SERVES 2

150 g (5 oz) natural yoghurt
  (3.5% fat)

100 g (3¹/₃ oz) cream cheese

1 tbsp tomato paste

2-3 tbsp milk

1 small tomato

½ small onion

½ bunch chives

salt, pepper

PREPARATION: about 15 mins

1. Blend the yoghurt with the cream cheese, the tomato paste and the milk.

2. Wash the tomato and remove the end. Peel the onion. Finely chop the tomato and the onion and fold both into the yoghurt mixture.

3. Wash and shake dry the chives, then chop them into thin rings. Stir the chives into the tomato mixture and season with salt and pepper.

TIP

You can serve this fruity dip with some hearty Ham & Olive balls - but it is much more versatile. The dip is just as tasty with meats, fish and potatoes, or as a spread on bread.

NUTRITIONAL VALUES PER PORTION:

245 Cal • 14 g protein • 18 g fat • 5 g carbohydrate

Vegetable & Swiss Cheese Carpaccio

SERVES 2

1 tsp lemon juice (if tolerated)

½ tsp white vinegar

4 tsp grapeseed oil

1 tsp chopped dill

salt, white pepper

glucose

100 g (3⅓ oz) Swiss cheese, thinly
    sliced (or Emmental or Cheddar)

3 radishes

1 yellow capsicum (pepper)

1 zucchini (courgette)

PREPARATION: about 25 mins

MARINATING: about 30 mins

1. Whisk the lemon juice with vinegar, 2–3 teaspoons water and the oil. Stir in the dill. Season with salt, pepper and glucose.

2. Cut the cheese into 2 cm (¾ in) diamonds. Stir the cheese into the marinade.

3. Wash and trim the radishes, then cut into thin slices. Halve, deseed and wash the capsicum, then cut into 2 cm (¾ in) diamonds. Wash and trim the zucchini, halve lengthways and cut into thin slices.

4. Gently fold the vegetable pieces into the cheese mixture. Leave to marinate for about 30 minutes. Divide the carpaccio between two plates and serve.

NUTRITIONAL VALUES PER PORTION:
285 Cal • 17 g protein • 21 g fat • 6 g carbohydrate

Yoghurt & Avocado Cream

SERVES 2

1 lemon

250 g (8 oz) natural yoghurt

1 tsp glucose

1 ripe avocado

salt, pepper

PREPARATION: about 15 mins

1. Squeeze the lemon. Whisk the juice with the yoghurt and the glucose.

2. Halve the avocado lengthways and remove the stone. Remove the flesh with a spoon, then finely mash with a fork.

3. Immediately fold the avocado paste into the yoghurt mixture. Generously season the avocado cream with salt and pepper to taste.

> **TIP**
> Thanks to its high fat content, this avocado cream is usually well tolerated even during the abstention phase – despite containing lemon juice. The avocado flesh quickly turns brown when it is exposed to air. Make sure therefore that you prepare the yoghurt cream first, then the avocado purée. Quickly blended, the cream will keep its attractive colour.

NUTRITIONAL VALUES PER PORTION:

370 Cal • 7 g protein • 34 g fat • 10 g carbohydrate

Curried Orange Dip

SERVES 2

125 g (4 oz) cream cheese

125 g (4 oz) natural yoghurt

50 ml (2 fl oz/¼ cup) orange juice

½ tsp honey

1 small garlic clove, peeled
   and crushed

salt, curry powder

PREPARATION: about 15 mins

1. Whisk the cream cheese with yoghurt, orange juice and honey.

2. Add the crushed garlic to the cheese mixture. Generously season the dip with salt and curry powder.

> **TIP**
> The Curried Orange Dip goes well with chicken and rice dishes. It also makes a great snack with carrot sticks. During the abstention phase, simply replace the honey with a little glucose.

NUTRITIONAL VALUES PER PORTION:

125 Cal • 10 g protein • 5 g fat • 9 g carbohydrate

Potato & Ham Muffins

MAKES 12 MUFFINS

200 g (6½ oz) potatoes

salt

200 g (6½ oz) plain flour

2 tsp baking powder

100 g (3⅓ oz) butter

1 onion

100 g (3⅓ oz) ham

1 egg

pepper, grated nutmeg

150 ml (5 fl oz/¾ cup) milk

PREPARATION: about 20 mins

BAKING: about 20 mins

1. Wash and peel the potatoes. Cook them in salted water for about 15–20 minutes. Drain and leave to cool, then roughly grate the potatoes.

2. Preheat the oven to 200°C/180°C fan-forced (middle shelf). Line a 12-hole muffin tray with paper cases. Combine the flour and the baking powder.

3. Melt the butter and pour into the flour mixture. Peel and finely chop the onion. Cut the ham into small dice. Add the onion, ham, potatoes and egg into the flour mixture and stir to combine. Season with salt, pepper and nutmeg.

4. Using a wooden spoon, beat the milk into the flour mixture until you have a sticky dough. Spoon the dough into the paper cases. Bake in the oven for about 20 minutes.

5. Leave the muffins in the tray to cool for 5 minutes. Take them out and place on a wire rack to cool completely.

TIP

Don't worry if you haven't got a muffin tray. Simply stack 2-3 paper cases inside one other on a tray.

NUTRITIONAL VALUES PER PORTION:

155 Cal • 5 g protein • 8 g fat • 15 g carbohydrate

Vegetable Waffles

SERVES 2

100 g (3⅓ oz) potatoes

250 g (8 oz) carrots

1 small zucchini (courgette)

1 small onion

2 eggs

2 tbsp wholemeal flour
    (about 50 g/1⅔ oz)

1 tbsp cornflour (cornstarch)

salt, pepper

½ tsp ground ginger

butter, for greasing

PREPARATION: about 45 mins

1. Wash and peel the potatoes. Trim and thinly peel the carrots. Wash and trim the zucchini. Grate the vegetables into thin strips.

2. Peel and finely chop the onion and stir into the vegetables.

3. Using a hand-held blender, whisk the eggs, flour and cornflour into the vegetable mixture. Generously season the batter with salt, pepper and ginger, then leave the batter to rise for about 25 minutes.

4. Preheat the waffle iron on a weak to moderate heat. Thinly grease the baking surfaces. Put 3 tablespoons batter into the middle of the lower baking surface. Squeeze down lightly, then close the waffle iron. One at a time, cook the waffles slowly until crisp and golden. Place them on a rack and continue until all the batter is used up.

TIP

These waffles are tasty at any time, whether eaten hot or cold, and they are extra tasty with a Yoghurt Salad Cream (see page 49). Choose a low temperature setting on the waffle iron, even if it takes a little longer – it will make the waffles easier to digest.

NUTRITIONAL VALUES PER WAFFLE:

245 Cal • 12 g protein • 6 g fat • 36 g carbohydrate

Broccoli Flan

**MAKES 12 SLICES
(1 LOOSE-BOTTOMED TIN,
26 CM/10 IN DIAMETER)**

butter, for greasing

150 g (5 oz) broccoli

100 g (3¹⁄₃ oz) soft butter

200 g (6½ oz) flour

4 tbsp milk

salt

flour, for dusting

200 g (6½ oz) cherry tomatoes

250 g (8 oz) sour cream

200 g (6½ oz) cream cheese

3 eggs

white pepper

PREPARATION: about 20 mins

BAKING: about 55 mins

1. Preheat the oven to 200°C/180°C fan-forced (middle shelf). Grease the tin. Leave the broccoli to thaw slightly.

2. Beat the butter until pale. Add flour, milk and salt; knead until you have a smooth dough.

3. Dust the work surface with flour; thinly roll out the dough. Place in the tin, forming a 2 cm (¾ in) edge. Prick the dough several times with a fork. Bake in the oven for 15 minutes.

4. Separate the broccoli into small florets and distribute them evenly over the flan base. Wash and halve the tomatoes and arrange in between the florets.

5. Whisk together the sour cream, cream cheese and eggs. Season with salt and pepper and pour the mixture over the vegetables. Bake the flan in the oven for 30–40 minutes, until the egg mixture has set and is golden. When inserted, a skewer should come out clean.

TIP

This broccoli flan looks great – and tastes even better. You can make it with other vegetables too. Thanks to the shortcrust pastry and the egg mixture used here, the flan is well tolerated even during the abstention phase. You can easily make it ahead of time and it tastes great hot or cold.

NUTRITIONAL VALUES PER PORTION:
245 Cal • 6 g protein • 18 g fat • 14 g carbohydrate

Spinach with Gorgonzola Cream

SERVES 2

1 shallot

1 tbsp oil

375 g (12 oz) frozen spinach

salt, white pepper, grated nutmeg

70 g (2½ oz) Gorgonzola

5 tbsp cream

2-3 tbsp white wine

PREPARATION: about 10 mins

1. Peel and finely chop the shallot.

2. Heat the oil in a wide saucepan, add the spinach and thaw, stirring constantly. Stir in the shallot. Cook the vegetables for about 10 minutes, until all the liquid has evaporated. Season with salt, pepper and nutmeg to taste.

3. Cut the Gorgonzola into dice. Heat the cream together with the wine. Stir in the cheese and let it melt. Season with pepper.

4. Divide the spinach and the Gorgonzola cream between plates and serve.

TIP

This vegetable dish is very quickly prepared. Serve it with a few slices of fresh white bread. Equally tasty is a side dish of narrow ribbon pasta. During the abstention phase you can replace the wine with vegetable stock. Sheep's cheese (minimum 60% fat) makes a delicious change from the Gorgonzola.

NUTRITIONAL VALUES PER PORTION:

290 Cal • 12 g protein • 24 g fat • 5 g carbohydrate

Fluffy Potato Bake

SERVES 2

500 g (1 lb) potatoes

butter, for greasing

2 eggs

salt, pepper

sweet paprika

grated nutmeg

100 g (3¹/₃ oz) cream

50 g (1²/₃ oz) butter

40 g (1½ oz) grated Emmental cheese

1-2 tsp breadcrumbs

PREPARATION: about 25 mins

BAKING: about 35 mins

1. Wash and peel the potatoes. Cook in salted water, covered, for about 20 minutes, then drain. Preheat the oven to 200°C/180°C fan-forced (middle shelf). Grease an ovenproof dish.

2. Separate the eggs. Beat the egg whites until stiff. Stir the egg yolks and season with salt, pepper, paprika and nutmeg.

3. Mash the hot potatoes using a hand-held blender. Add the cream, 40 g (1½ oz) butter and cheese, and stir until you have a creamy purée. First stir in the egg yolk mixture, then gently fold in the egg white foam.

4. Spread the potato purée evenly in the dish. Sprinkle lightly with breadcrumbs. Make small pats of the remaining butter and place on top. Bake 35 minutes until golden.

SERVE WITH

If you like, serve a refreshing green mixed-leaf salad with this potato bake.

NUTRITIONAL VALUES PER PORTION:

665 Cal • 18 g protein • 48 g fat • 39 g carbohydrate

Spinach Lasagne

SERVES 2

1 chicken breast fillet
(about 150 g/5 oz)

1 onion

1 small garlic clove

1 tbsp oil

500 g (1 lb) frozen spinach

100 g (3¹/₃ oz) cream cheese
with herbs

75 ml (2½ fl oz/¹/₃ cup) milk

salt pepper, grated nutmeg

1 level tsp instant vegetable
stock granules

4 lasagne sheets

50 g (1²/₃ oz) grated cheese
(e.g. Emmental)

PREPARATION: about 30 mins

BAKING: about 35 mins

1. Rinse the meat and pat dry, then cut into thin strips. Peel and finely chop the onion and garlic.

2. Heat the oil and fry the onion and garlic for a few minutes. Add the chicken and fry, stirring, until browned all over. Add the spinach, cover and cook for about 15 minutes, until the leaves have thawed. Stir in the cream cheese and the milk. Season generously with salt, pepper, nutmeg and the instant stock granules.

3. Preheat the oven to 220°C/200°C fan-forced (middle shelf). Place one-third of the spinach mixture into the dish. Cover with 2 lasagne sheets. Add another third of spinach and 2 more lasagne sheets. Place the last third of spinach on top.

4. Sprinkle the lasagne with cheese and cook in the oven for about 35 minutes until golden.

TIP

Another delicious idea: use 150 g (5 oz) diced feta instead of the chicken breast but only stir this in when the vegetables are cooked. Make sure that the lasagne finishes with spinach to let the pasta sheets swell.

NUTRITIONAL VALUES PER PORTION:
565 Cal • 40 g protein • 27 g fat • 40 g carbohydrate

Ribbon Pasta with mushrooms and pine nuts

SERVES 2

1 tsp dried porcini

200 g (6½ oz) fresh or dried
chanterelles (or other mushrooms)

1 shallot

1 tbsp oil

75 g (2¾ oz) sour cream

salt, pepper, dried marjoram

25 g (¾ oz) pine nuts

200 g (6½ oz) ribbon pasta

PREPARATION: about 30 mins

VARIATION

If chanterelles are not available, simply make the mushroom sauce using 200 g (6½ oz) button mushrooms.

1. Cook the pasta in boiling salted water according to packet instructions until al dente (firm to the bite).

2. Rinse the porcini under cold water. Pour over 100 ml (3 fl oz/ ½ cup) hot water and leave to swell for 10 minutes. Brush and trim the chanterelles. Peel and finely chop the shallot.

3. Heat the oil and fry the shallot. Sprinkle in the chanterelles and fry briefly. Take the porcini out of the soaking water and finely chop them, reserving the liquid. Stir the porcini into the pan and cook for a further 5 minutes.

4. Stir the sour cream and 2–3 tablespoons reserved mushroom water into the vegetables. Season with salt, pepper and marjoram. Dry-roast the pine kernels over medium heat in a non-stick pan until golden.

5. Drain the pasta. Arrange on plates with the mushrooms. Sprinkle with the pine nuts.

NUTRITIONAL VALUES PER PORTION:
600 Cal • 17 g protein • 23 g fat • 80 g carbohydrate

Meaty Mexican Tortillas

SERVES 2

FOR THE BATTER

75 g (2¾ oz) polenta

1 heaped tbsp plain flour
(25 g/¾ oz)

salt

250 ml (8 fl oz/1 cup) milk

2 eggs

1 tsp butter

oil, for deep-frying

FOR THE FILLING

125 g (4 oz) red kidney
beans (tinned)

2 small tomatoes

1 small onion

1 small garlic clove

1 tsp oil

150 g (5 oz) minced beef

3 tsp tomato paste

salt, chilli powder

PREPARATION: about 45 mins

1. To make the batter, combine the polenta with the flour and salt. Slowly beat in the milk, using a whisk, until you have a thin and liquid batter. Vigorously beat in the eggs. Melt the butter and stir into the batter.

2. Heat a little oil in a non-stick pan (24 cm/9½ in diameter). Add a ladle of batter and spread it evenly in the pan. Cook the pancake over medium heat for 1–2 minutes. Turn and briefly cook the other side. Let the finished pancake glide onto a plate. Cook another 3 thin pancakes in the same way.

3. To make the filling, drain the beans. Wash the tomatoes, remove the ends and finely dice the flesh. Peel and finely chop the onion and the garlic.

4. Heat the oil and fry the onion and the garlic. Stir in the minced meat and fry until it is browned all over. Stir in the beans, the tomatoes and the tomato paste. Cook for about 5 minutes. Season to taste with salt and chilli powder.

5. Spread a few spoonfuls of the minced meat sauce on each tortilla pancake and roll them up. Serve immediately.

SERVE WITH

These tortillas are delicious with a fresh Yoghurt & Avocado Cream (see page 59).

NUTRITIONAL VALUES PER PORTION:
820 Cal • 45 g protein • 35 g fat • 81 g carbohydrate

Risi e Bisi (rice with peas)

SERVES 2

1 small onion

2 tbsp olive oil

250 g (8 oz) long-grain rice
(parboiled)

125 g (4 oz) peas (fresh or frozen)

1 tsp salt

PREPARATION: about 30 mins

1. Peel and finely chop the onion.

2. Heat the oil in a saucepan and fry the onion for a few minutes. Stir in the rice and sauté until it is translucent.

3. Pour in 500 ml (16 fl oz/2 cups) water. Stir in the peas and the salt and bring to the boil. Turn off the heat, cover and leave the rice to swell for about 25 minutes, until it has soaked up all the water.

TIP

This quickly cooked rice dish is sufficient for two people as a main course or for four as a side dish, served with grilled meat. Children usually love this simple dish.

NUTRITIONAL VALUES PER PORTION:

570 Cal • 12 g protein • 11 g fat • 106 g carbohydrate

Veggie Rice with cashew nuts

SERVES 2

100 g (3¹/₃ oz) Basmati rice

salt

150 g (5 oz) carrots

150 g (5 oz) zucchini (courgettes)

3 tsp oil

75 g (2¾ oz) cashew nuts

pepper, curry powder

PREPARATION: about 30 mins

1. In a large saucepan, sprinkle the rice into 250 ml (8 fl oz/1 cup) boiling salted water, cover the pan and cook over low heat for 15 minutes.

2. Trim and thinly peel the carrots. Wash and trim the zucchini. Cut both into short strips. Heat the oil in a large pan or a wok and fry the carrots over medium heat for 5 minutes. Stir in the zucchini and fry the vegetables for a further 5 minutes.

3. Dry-roast the cashew nuts in a non-stick frying pan without fat over low heat, stirring constantly, until they are golden.

4. Fold the rice and cashews into the vegetables. Season generously with salt, pepper and curry powder.

TIP

If you prefer capsicums and button mushrooms, simply prepare this stir-fry dish with your favourite vegetables. If you like, serve with the Curried Orange Dip (see page 59).

NUTRITIONAL VALUES PER PORTION:

480 Cal • 11 g protein • 24 g fat • 55 g carbohydrate

Baked Salmon with herbs

SERVES 2

2 salmon fillets
    (about 200 g/6½ oz)
½ lemon
2 small spring onions
½ bunch mixed herbs
    (e.g. parsley,
    chives, basil)
salt, curry powder
1 egg white

PREPARATION: about 15 mins
MARINATING: about 2 hrs
COOKING: about 15 mins

1. Rinse the fish under cold water and pat dry with kitchen paper. Cut into large pieces. Squeeze out the lemon and drizzle the juice over the fish.

2. Wash and trim the spring onions, then chop, including the green parts. Wash, shake dry and finely chop the herbs. Combine both with the fish. Season with salt and curry powder, cover and leave for 1–2 hours in the fridge to marinate.

3. Preheat the oven to 220°C/200°C fan-forced (middle shelf). Line a baking tray with baking paper. Whisk the egg white until stiff. Coat the fish pieces in the egg until covered all over, then place on the baking tray.

4. Bake the salmon in the oven for about 15 minutes until it is golden. Serve with oven-baked potatoes or a baguette.

OILY FISH

Salmon is particularly rich in valuable healthy fats. It contains omega-3 fatty acids which prevent heart and circulatory diseases and inhibit inflammations. Herring, tuna and mackerel are all similarly healthy.

NUTRITIONAL VALUES PER PORTION:
425 Cal • 42 g protein • 27 g fat • 2 g carbohydrate

Ling Fish on mustard vegetables

SERVES 2

2 ling (150 g/5 oz each)
½ lemon
½ leek
1 carrot (100 g/3⅓ oz)
75 g (2¾ oz) celeriac
1 tbsp oil
50 ml (2 fl oz/¼ cup)
    vegetable stock
salt, pepper
100 g (3⅓ oz) sour cream
1 tsp mustard

PREPARATION: about 35 mins

1. Rinse the fish under cold water; pat dry with kitchen paper. Squeeze the lemon and drizzle the juice over the fish.

2. Trim the leek, halve it lengthways and wash thoroughly. Cut into thin rings. Trim and peel the carrot and the celeriac and cut into thin sticks.

3. Heat the oil in a wide saucepan and sauté the vegetables for 2 minutes. Pour in the stock and bring to the boil.

4. Season the fish with salt and pepper and place on top of the vegetables. Cover and cook over low to medium heat for 10 minutes. Carefully lift out the fish.

5. Stir the sour cream and mustard into the vegetables. Season with salt and pepper. Arrange the mustard vegetables and the fish on plates. Serve with white bread or rice.

LEMON AND FISH

You can only acidulate fish with fresh lemon juice. Artificial concentrate does not have any effect on the fish protein. Both fish dishes are, however, well tolerated even in the abstention phase, for the lemon juice is not used in the actual cooking of the fish.

NUTRITIONAL VALUES PER PORTION:
320 Cal • 31 g protein • 19 g fat • 7 g carbohydrate

Italian-style Tomato Chicken

SERVES 4

150 g (5 oz) shallots

3 garlic cloves

1 small chicken or poussin
   (1.5 kg/3 lb 6 oz)

salt, black pepper

4 tbsp oil

3 small sprigs rosemary

4 bay leaves

3 small tins (200 g/6½ oz each)
   peeled tomatoes (drained weight
   480 g/15½ oz in total)

80 g (2¾ oz) black olives

PREPARATION: about 40 mins

COOKING: about 40 mins

1. Preheat the oven to 250°C/230°C fan-forced (middle shelf). Peel the shallots and the garlic. Halve the shallots, and finely chop the garlic.

2. Wash and pat dry the chicken. Cut off the legs. Cut the body in half lengthways using poultry scissors. Season the chicken pieces all over with salt and pepper.

3. Heat the oil in a roasting tin. Quickly fry the chicken pieces all over until browned. Add the shallots and the garlic. Wash and pat dry the rosemary. Stir in the rosemary with the bay leaves and tomatoes. Bring to the boil. Season with salt and pepper. Add the olives to the chicken.

4. Cover with a lid and roast in the oven for 30 minutes. Reduce the temperature to 200°C/180°C fan-forced. Uncover, and cook the chicken for about 10 minutes more, until it is crispy and brown on the outside. Serve immediately.

TIP

Simply serve the Tomato Chicken with some Italian ciabatta bread. This bread is great for dunking in the delicious sauce. If you're in a hurry, just prepare the dish using 4 chicken breast fillets. Cook them at 200°C/180°C fan-forced (middle shelf) for only 25 minutes in the oven, leaving the roasting tin uncovered.

NUTRITIONAL VALUES PER PORTION:
770 Cal • 58 g protein • 54 g fat • 13 g carbohydrate

Baked Chicken Breast with herbed potatoes

SERVES 2

500 g (1 lb) potatoes
1 small sprig thyme
1 small sprig rosemary
2 tbsp oil
1 garlic clove, peeled and crushed
2 chicken breast fillets
salt, pepper
1 tbsp tomato sauce
1 tsp honey
3 tsp soy sauce
125 ml (4 fl oz/½ cup)
   vegetable stock
400 g (13 oz) tomatoes
1 onion
PREPARATION: about 20 mins
COOKING: about 55 mins

1. Wash and thoroughly scrub the potatoes. Peel those that have a very hard skin. Halve the larger ones. Spread the potatoes in a large baking dish. Preheat the oven to 200°C/180°C fan-forced (middle shelf).

2. Wash and pat dry the thyme and the rosemary. Chop the leaves and needles; stir them into the oil. Add the crushed garlic to the mixture. Drizzle the herb oil over the potatoes.

3. Rinse the chicken under cold water and pat dry. Season with salt and pepper and place the pieces in between the potatoes. Whisk together the tomato sauce, honey and soy sauce. Briefly bring the marinade to the boil, then brush over the fillets.

4. Pour in the stock. Cook in the oven for 40 minutes, turning the potatoes once.

5. Wash the tomatoes and remove the ends. Halve or quarter tomatoes depending on their size. Peel the onion and cut into rings. Place tomatoes and onion rings in between the potatoes. Continue cooking in the oven for about 15 minutes.

6. Divide the chicken, potatoes and tomatoes between plates and serve immediately.

TIP

Be careful when buying tomato sauce! Make sure the sauce contains glucose or glucose syrup rather than fructose or fructose syrup. Tomato sauces for children often contain fructose, although they are often advertised as "free from granulated sugar".

NUTRITIONAL VALUES PER PORTION:
555 Cal • 64 g protein • 13 g fat • 46 g carbohydrate

Turkey & Vegetable Kebabs

SERVES 2

250 g (8 oz) turkey escalopes

2 tbsp oil

3 tbsp soy sauce

2 tbsp tomato sauce

1 tsp mustard

salt, pepper

100 g (3^{1}/$_{3}$ oz) small button
  mushrooms

1 small zucchini (courgette)

½ yellow capsicum (pepper)

100 g (3^{1}/$_{3}$ oz) cherry tomatoes

PREPARATION: about 40 mins

GRILLING: about 12 mins

1. Rinse the meat under cold water, pat dry with kitchen paper and chop into large pieces.

2. Whisk the oil with the soy sauce, tomato sauce, mustard, salt and pepper. Drizzle the marinade over the meat.

3. Clean the mushrooms with a dry brush and trim them. Wash and trim zucchini and capsicum, then cut them into chunks. Wash and halve the tomatoes.

4. Preheat an oven with a grill to 180°C/160°C fan-forced (middle shelf). Line a baking tray with baking paper. Alternating, thread kebab sticks with meat pieces, mushrooms, vegetable chunks and tomato halves. Brush the vegetables with the remaining marinade.

5. Place the kebab sticks on the tray and grill them in the oven for 5–6 minutes. Turn over and grill for another 5–6 minutes. Serve the kebabs with ribbon pasta or ciabatta bread.

> **TIP**
>
> Children often enjoy threading the skewers themselves. Let them choose their vegetables and create their own colour sequence.

NUTRITIONAL VALUES PER PORTION:

285 Cal • 34 g protein • 12 g fat • 11 g carbohydrate

Ginger and Turkey Pot with herbs

SERVES 2

375 g (13 oz) turkey escalopes

1 tsp sesame oil

150 g (5 oz) spring onions

125 ml (4 fl oz/½ cup)
  vegetable stock

1 piece fresh ginger
  (about 2 cm/½ in)

pepper

1 tbsp soy sauce

¼ bunch parsley

PREPARATION: about 35 mins

1. Rinse the meat under cold water, pat dry with kitchen paper and cut into dice.

2. Heat the oil in a wide saucepan. Quickly fry the meat all over until brown.

3. Wash and trim the spring onions, then cut into thin rings. Stir into the meat pan and fry for a further 3 minutes. Pour in the stock. Cover and leave to braise over low heat for about 20 minutes.

4. Peel the ginger and grate over the turkey with a fine grater. Season to taste with pepper and soy sauce.

5. Wash and shake dry, then finely chop the parsley. Divide the pot between plates and sprinkle with the parsley. Serve with basmati rice.

NUTRITIONAL VALUES PER PORTION:

240 Cal • 47 g protein • 4 g fat • 4 g carbohydrate

Colourful Meatloaf

MAKES 16 SLICES
(1 LOAF TIN, 30 CM/12 IN)

3 gherkins

2 marinated green capsicums
(pepper, about 70 g/2½ oz,
from the jar)

4 sundried tomatoes in oil (about
100 g/3¹/₃ oz, from the jar)

1 kg (2 lb 4 oz) minced meat
(beef and pork)

2 eggs

3 tbsp oat bran flakes

20 pitted black olives

2 tsp Dijon mustard

salt, pepper

PREPARATION: about 10 mins

COOKING: about 40 mins

1. Drain the gherkins, marinated capsicum and tomatoes.

2. Combine the minced meat with the eggs and the oat bran flakes. Preheat the oven to 180°C/160°C fan-forced (middle shelf).

3. Cut the gherkins, capsicum and tomatoes into small dice. Cut the olives into thin slices. Stir all into the minced meat mixture. Stir in the mustard. Generously season the meat mixture with salt and pepper to taste.

4. Evenly spread the meat mixture into a loaf tin. Cook in the oven for about 40 minutes.

5. Cut the meat loaf into slices while hot and serve in the loaf tin or on a serving dish. Serve with mashed potatoes, if desired.

PARTY FUN

If you're expecting guests, why not cook the meat loaf in a round cake tin? Leave the loaf to cool a little, then turn it out of the dish and place it on the buffet table, to eat hot or cold.

VARIATION

Cheese lovers could chop 75 g (2¾ oz) firm sheep's cheese (45% fat) and stir into the minced meat mixture.

NUTRITIONAL VALUES PER PORTION:
200 Cal • 15 g protein • 14 g fat • 4 g carbohydrate

Pork Fillet on a bed of vegetables

SERVES 2

250 g (8 oz) carrots

¼ celeriac

200 g (6½ oz) zucchini (courgette)

200 g (6½ oz) broccoli

1 onion

250 g (8 oz) pork fillet

salt, white pepper

1 tbsp margarine

250 ml (8 fl oz/1 cup)
    vegetable stock

1 tbsp mustard

1 tsp dried mixed herbs

½ box mustard cress

PREPARATION: about 35 mins

ROASTING: about 25 mins

1. Trim and thinly peel the carrots and the celeriac, then cut into thin strips. Wash and trim the zucchini, then cut into 1 cm (½ in) slices. Separate the broccoli florets. Peel and finely chop the onion.

2. Preheat the oven to 200°C/180°C fan-forced (middle shelf). Pat dry the meat with kitchen paper. Season all over with salt and pepper. Heat the margarine in a roasting pan and fry the fillet all over until browned. Remove and set aside.

3. Stir the onion into the roasting juices and cook until translucent. Stir in the vegetables and pour in the stock. Season with salt and pepper.

4. Stir together the mustard and mixed herbs. Spread the mustard mixture all over the pork. Place the meat on top of the vegetables, cover and roast for about 25 minutes in the oven.

5. Rinse and shake dry the cress, then cut off the leaves. Divide the fillet between plates and sprinkle with the cress. Serve with jacket potatoes.

TIP

You can use different vegetables for this dish depending on what you can tolerate. For example, try cauliflower, pointed cabbage or capsicum.

NUTRITIONAL VALUES PER PORTION:

285 Cal • 35 g protein • 11 g fat • 12 g carbohydrate

Pork Fillet Parcels with prosciutto and melted cheese

SERVES 2

250 g (8 oz) pork fillet
75 g (2¾ oz) prosciutto
100 g (3⅓ oz) sour cream
50 ml (2 fl oz/¼ cup) milk
50 g (1⅔ oz) blue vein cheese
salt, pepper
PREPARATION: about 20 mins
ROASTING: about 20 mins

1. Preheat the oven to 170°C/150°C fan-forced (middle shelf). Pat the meat dry with kitchen paper. Divide every fillet into four pieces.

2. Wrap each fillet piece in a slice of prosciutto. Place the fillet parcels next to each other in a baking dish. Bake in the oven for 15 minutes until cooked.

3. In a small saucepan, whisk the sour cream with the milk. Warm through over medium heat. Dice the cheese and let it melt in the sauce. Season the cheese sauce with salt and pepper.

4. Spread the cheese sauce over the fillet parcels. Continue cooking the parcels for about 5 minutes until golden.

5. Place 2 fillet parcels on each plate. Serve immediately, with ribbon pasta or potatoes.

VARIATION

To make Saltimbocca, place a few fresh sage leaves on top of 4 small veal escalopes (250 g/8 oz) and wrap with the prosciutto. Continue cooking as per the recipe.

NUTRITIONAL VALUES PER PORTION:
500 Cal • 41 g protein • 36 g fat • 3 g carbohydrate

Crunchy Meat Patties

SERVES 2

½ bunch flat-leaf parsley

50 g (1²/₃ oz) peanuts

1 small onion

250 g (8 oz) minced beef

1 small egg

salt, black pepper

sweet paprika

1 tsp soy sauce

1-2 tsp oat bran flakes

ghee (clarified butter), for frying

PREPARATION: about 25 mins

1. Wash and shake dry the parsley. Chop the parsley and the peanuts. Peel and finely chop the onion.

2. Combine the minced meat and the egg. Stir in the parsley and peanut mixture and the onion. Season with salt, pepper, paprika and soy sauce. Stir in the oat bran flakes.

3. With moistened hands, form the minced meat mixture into 8 flat burger shapes.

4. Heat the ghee in a frying pan. Fry the burgers for 5–6 minutes on each side until brown. Lift them out and divide between plates. The patties go well with French fries or jacket potatoes.

TIP

Children love these crunchy nutty meat patties, they are always a great hit at children's parties.

VARIATION

Are you a fan of all things Mexican? How about Filled Tacos? For these, season the minced meat with 1 teaspoon ground cumin instead of the soy sauce. In a frying pan, heat a little oil and fry the meat until it is crumbly. Cut ¼ iceberg lettuce (or 1 Romana lettuce heart) into strips and divide between 2 taco shells. Add the hot meat mixture and a dab of sour cream on each taco. Serve immediately.

NUTRITIONAL VALUES PER PORTION:

460 Cal • 38 g protein • 32 g fat • 5 g carbohydrate

Beef Stir-Fry with snowpeas

SERVES 2

200 g (6½ oz) lean beef fillet

1 piece fresh ginger (2 cm/¾ in)

2½ tsp soy sauce

100 g (3⅓ oz) snowpeas
   (mangetout)

½ small yellow capsicum (pepper)

1 level tsp cornflour (cornstarch)

60 ml (2 fl oz/¼ cup) beef stock

2 tsp soybean oil (or vegetable oil)

½ tsp dark sesame oil

PREPARATION: about 25 mins

MARINATING: about 30 mins

1. Pat the meat dry with some kitchen paper and cut into thin strips. Peel and finely grate the ginger. Combine the meat with 2 teaspoons soy sauce and the ginger, and leave to marinate for about 30 minutes.

2. Meanwhile trim the snowpeas and cut in half. Wash the capsicum, then cut into thin sticks. Stir the cornflour into 3 teaspoons stock; set aside.

3. Heat a frying pan and pour in the soy oil. Fry the meat over high heat for about 2 minutes with the marinade. Add the snowpeas and capsicum sticks and fry, stirring constantly, for 2 minutes. Pour in the remaining stock and the soy sauce, sesame oil and the dissolved cornflour. Briefly heat through, until the sauce binds together.

4. Divide the beef between two plates. Serve with a bowl of steaming basmati rice.

AUTHENTIC

It is best to cook this beef dish in a wok – but not everyone owns one. Alternatively use a frying pan instead. Try and use the dark sesame oil as it adds a particular flavour to this dish.

VARIATION

Put the flavour of Asia onto your table. Finely chop the white parts of 2 sticks lemon grass. Cut the green parts into 3 cm (1¼ in) lengths. Combine the chopped lemon grass with 100 g (3⅓ oz) cooked shelled prawns (fresh or frozen), ginger and soy sauce and combine with the beef fillet strips. Leave to marinate for 30 minutes. Meanwhile, fry the green lemon grass pieces together with the other vegetables, then continue as per the recipe.

NUTRITIONAL VALUES PER PORTION:

190 Cal • 23 g protein • 8 g fat • 5 g carbohydrate

Raspberries with mascarpone and pine nuts

SERVES 2

125 g (4 oz) raspberries
  (fresh or frozen)
125 g (4 oz) mascarpone
100 g (3⅓ oz) natural yoghurt
50 g (1⅔ oz) dextrose
½ vanilla pod
ground cinnamon
2 tbsp pine nuts

PREPARATION: about 25 mins

1. Carefully wash and drain the raspberries. Leave the frozen fruit to thaw. Divide the berries between two serving bowls.

2. Stir together the mascarpone, yoghurt and dextrose. Slit the vanilla pod lengthways and scrape out the seeds. Stir into the mascarpone cream.

3. Divide the cream equally between the bowls and dust with the cinnamon.

4. Dry-roast the pine nuts in a non-stick pan without fat over medium heat, stirring constantly, until golden. Sprinkle the nuts over the cream and top with the extra raspberries.

TIP

For a change, make this dessert with other berries you can tolerate, for example blueberries, blackberries or a mixture of different kinds. This mascarpone cream is particularly delicious if topped with almond brittle (see page 114).

VARIATION

Create a Tiramisu in the Glass with this mascarpone cream. Make the cream as per the recipe on this page. Into 1 double espresso stir 1 teaspoon dextrose and 2 drops almond extract. Drizzle the mixture over 60 g (2 oz) cornflakes. Layer the cereal in two glasses, alternating with the mascarpone cream. Dust with cocoa and serve immediately. If you desire – and can tolerate it – you could also add a dash of almond liqueur (Amaretto) or orange liqueur (Cointreau) to the espresso.

NUTRITIONAL VALUES PER PORTION:
500 Cal • 7 g protein • 38 g fat • 34 g carbohydrate

Sweet Donuts with cherry sauce

SERVES 4
FOR THE DOUGH
250 g (8 oz) plain flour
110 g (4 oz) dextrose
20 g (²/₃ oz) fresh yeast
  or 2 tsp dried yeast
60 ml (2 fl oz/¼ cup) warm milk
60 g (2 oz) soft butter, 1 egg
butter, for greasing
flour, for dusting
FOR THE SAUCE
300 g (10 oz) morello cherries
  (from the jar)
5 tbsp cherry juice (from the jar)
1 tbsp kirsch (if desired)
1 tsp balsamic vinegar
1 tbsp icing sugar
PREPARATION: about 40 mins
RESTING: about 1 hr
BAKING: about 15 mins

1. For the dough combine the flour with 35 g (1¼ oz) dextrose. Make a hollow in the centre, crumble in the yeast and pour in the milk. Stir, using the dough hooks of the hand-held blender. Add the butter and the egg and knead for 3 minutes to form a smooth dough.

2. Cover the dough and leave to rise in a warm place for about 30 minutes, until doubled in volume. Grease an ovenproof dish.

3. Preheat the oven to 70°C/50°C fan-forced. Knead through the dough once more, then roll it out 1 cm (½ in) thick on a floured work surface. Cut out circles (4 cm/1½ in diameter) and place in the dish, leaving space in between.

4. Warm the circles in the oven for 5 minutes. Turn off the heat and leave the circles for about 30 minutes to double in size. Reheat the oven to 170°C/150°C fan-forced (middle shelf) and bake the donuts for about 15 minutes until golden.

5. To make the sauce, purée the cherries, the juice and the rest of the dextrose in the mixer or with a hand-held blender. Flavour with kirsch and vinegar and distribute on four dessert plates.

6. Place the donuts on top of the cherry sauce and dust with icing sugar to serve.

NUTRITIONAL VALUES PER PORTION:
515 Cal • 10 g protein • 15 g fat • 82 g carbohydrate

Cream Cheese Blinis

SERVES 2
25 g (¾ oz) soft butter
20 g (²/₃ oz) dextrose
1 tsp lemon flavour (alternatively
  grated zest of an organic lemon)
2 eggs
250 g (8 oz) low-fat cream cheese
75 g (2¾ oz) plain flour
about 2 tbsp milk
margarine, for frying
PREPARATION: about 25 mins

1. Beat the butter with the dextrose and the lemon flavour until pale. Stir in the eggs, one at a time, and beat until you have a thick foam.

2. Stir in the cream cheese and the flour. Add enough milk to make a creamy batter.

3. Heat a little margarine in a frying pan. Drop in 2 tablespoons batter for each blini and flatten. Fry the blinis over medium heat on both sides until golden. Continue in the same way until all the batter is used up.

TIP
The blinis taste particularly delicious with the Vanilla Cherry Cream (see page 31) and the Chocolate Butter (see page 32), but you can also serve them with stewed fruit, such as the Rhubarb Compote (see page 96).

NUTRITIONAL VALUES PER PORTION:
425 Cal • 26 g protein • 17 g fat • 42 g carbohydrate

Yoghurt Mousse with berry sauce

SERVES 2

3 sheets white gelatine

1 tbsp lemon juice

2 tbsp + 100 g (3$^1/_3$ oz) dextrose

250 g (8 oz) creamy yoghurt

200 g (6½ oz) raspberries
(fresh or frozen)

1 tsp chopped pistachios

PREPARATION: about 35 mins

CHILLING: about 2 hrs

1. Soak the gelatine in cold water for 5 minutes. Whisk the lemon juice and 2 tablespoons dextrose into the yoghurt.

2. Squeeze out the gelatine and dissolve in a small saucepan over low heat. Stir in 2 tablespoons, then the remaining yoghurt cream. Chill the cream for about 2 hours.

3. Carefully wash and drain the fresh raspberries, or leave the frozen fruits to thaw.

4. Purée the berries with 100 g (3$^1/_3$ oz) dextrose in a mixer or using a hand-held blender. If desired, strain the purée through a fine sieve to remove the small raspberry seeds.

5. Divide the raspberry sauce between two dessert plates. Using a tablespoon, cut off scoops of the yoghurt mousse and place on top of the berry sauce. Sprinkle with pistachios.

FEAR OF GELATINE

Don't shy away from gelatine. The following tips will help you when using it:

- Never bring gelatine to the boil. Take it off the heat as soon as it has dissolved.
- Create a temperature balance: first stir a few spoonfuls of the cold mixture into the liquid gelatine, then slowly add the gelatine to the remaining cold mixture.
- If you want to play it completely safe for the first time, use 1–2 extra sheets gelatine than stated in a recipe. It's also best to increase the amount of gelatine on particularly hot days to help ensure it sets well.

VARIATION

For a change, make the sauce from blueberries, blackberries or a mixture of berries. Another particularly nice variation is a sauce or a salad made from fresh strawberries, sweetened with dextrose.

NUTRITIONAL VALUES PER PORTION:
385 Cal • 8 g protein • 5 g fat • 75 g carbohydrate

Rhubarb Compote with vanilla cream

SERVES 2-3

250 g (8 oz) rhubarb

65 g (oz) dextrose

¾ tsp liquid sweetener

½ packet vanilla custard powder
(for 500 ml/16 fl oz/2 cups milk)

250 ml (8 fl oz/1 cup) milk

100 g (3⅓ oz) low-fat
cream cheese

1 tbsp sour cream

3 tbsp flaked almonds

1 heaped tbsp sugar

PREPARATION: about 25 mins

1. Wash and trim the rhubarb, then cut into 1 cm (½ in) chunks. Cook together with 15 g (½ oz) dextrose and sweetener for about 5 minutes until soft. Divide between 2–3 dessert bowls and leave to cool.

2. Whisk the custard powder into 50 ml (2 fl oz/¼ cup) milk. Bring 200 ml (7 fl oz/¾ cup) milk and 50 g (1⅔ oz) dextrose to the boil. Stir in the dissolved custard powder and bring to the boil. Take the custard off the heat and leave to cool for about 10 minutes. Occasionally stir through with a whisk so that no skin starts to form on the surface.

3. Stir the cream cheese and the sour cream into the custard. Put the vanilla cream on top of the rhubarb compote.

4. Dry-roast the almonds and the sugar in a non-stick pan without fat over high heat, stirring, until the sugar caramelises and the almonds turn golden. Sprinkle with the almond brittle and serve.

TIP
If you don't fancy rhubarb, try making this dessert with raspberries. You can buy them frozen all year round.

NUTRITIONAL VALUES PER PORTION:
290 Cal • 10 g protein • 10 g fat • 41 g carbohydrate

Semolina Pudding with kiwi fruit

SERVES 2

250 ml (8 fl oz/1 cup) milk

3 tsp dextrose

½ tsp butter

30 g (1 oz) semolina

1 kiwi fruit

PREPARATION: about 40 mins

1. Bring the milk and the dextrose to the boil. Stir in the butter and the semolina and briefly bring back to the boil. Turn off the heat, cover and leave the semolina to swell for about 25 minutes. Stir occasionally so no skin starts to form.

2. Fill the semolina pudding into two dessert bowls. Leave to cool a little.

3. Peel the kiwi fruit and quarter lengthways. Garnish each pudding with 2 kiwi quarters. Serve immediately.

FRUITY
This pudding will also taste delicious with melon wedges, berries or peach slices.

NUTRITIONAL VALUES PER PORTION:
180 Cal • 6 g protein • 6 g fat • 26 g carbohydrate

Melon Cocktail with cinnamon cream cheese

SERVES 2

¼ honeydew melon

200 g (6½ oz) low-fat cream cheese

100 g (3⅓ oz) sour cream

50 g (1⅔ oz) + 1 tsp dextrose

¼ tsp cinnamon

PREPARATION: about 10 mins

1. Scoop out the seeds from the honeydew melon. Peel the fruit and chop the flesh into small dice. Place the melon dice into two cocktail glasses.

2. Stir together the cream cheese, the sour cream and 50 g (1⅔ oz) dextrose. Divide the cream on top of the fruits in the glasses.

3. Combine the cinnamon with 1 teaspoon dextrose, then sprinkle over the cream dessert.

NUTRITIONAL VALUES PER PORTION:

265 Cal • 16 g protein • 5 g fat • 39 g carbohydrate

Bananas in chocolate chilli sauce

SERVES 2

40 g (1½ oz) dark chocolate
   (70% cocoa)

50 ml (2 fl oz/¼ cup) milk

3 tsp dextrose

1 pinch cayenne pepper

2 bananas

1 tsp butter

PREPARATION: about 15 mins

1. Break the chocolate into squares. Heat up the milk. Add the chocolate and melt, stirring, over low heat. Stir in the dextrose and cayenne pepper.

2. Peel the bananas. Heat the butter in a frying pan, add the bananas and lightly fry on both sides over medium heat.

3. Place the bananas on two dessert plates. Pour over the hot chocolate sauce and serve immediately.

ANY OLD CHILLI?

Take care when choosing spices: ground chilli pods are known as cayenne pepper – not chilli powder. The latter may be a mixture of cayenne pepper, paprika, dried garlic and any number of other spices.

NUTRITIONAL VALUES PER PORTION:

260 Cal • 3 g protein • 11 g fat • 36 g carbohydrate

Chocolate Ice Cream

SERVES 4

1 very fresh egg yolk

100 g (3⅓ oz) dextrose

15 g (½ oz) cocoa

200 ml (7 fl oz/¾ cup) milk

150 g (5 oz) cream

25 g (¾ oz) dark chocolate
(70% cocoa)

PREPARATION: about 10 mins

CHILLING: about 40 mins

1. Whisk the egg yolk with the dextrose, cocoa and milk until the cocoa has dissolved.

2. Beat the cream until nearly stiff, then carefully fold into the cocoa mixture.

3. Coarsely chop the chocolate and fold into the cream. Stir the mixture in the ice cream maker for 40 minutes until you have a creamy, semi-soft ice cream.

TIP

Make sure you only use very fresh eggs for all ice cream recipes. If you want to do without eggs entirely, simply substitute an extra 50 g (1⅔ oz) cream for each egg yolk in a recipe.

VARIATION

If you like the flavour of nuts, stir an additional 40 g (1½ oz) chopped hazelnuts or 4 drops almond extract into the ice cream.

NUTRITIONAL VALUES PER PORTION:

310 Cal • 5 g protein • 18 g fat • 32 g carbohydrate

Creamy Vanilla Ice Cream

SERVES 4

4 very fresh egg yolks

100 g (3$\frac{1}{3}$ oz) dextrose

1 tsp ground Bourbon vanilla
(alternatively 2-3 drops
vanilla essence)

150 g (5 oz) cream

200 ml (7 fl oz/¾ cup) milk

PREPARATION: about 10 mins

CHILLING: about 40 mins

1. Beat the egg yolks, the dextrose and vanilla using a hand-held blender until thick and foamy.

2. Stir the cream and the milk into the egg mixture.

3. In the ice cream maker, stir the mixture for about 40 minutes until you have a creamy, semi-soft ice cream.

TIP

Don't worry if you haven't got an ice cream maker. Fill the ice cream mixture into a shallow dish, cover and place in the freezer. Stir vigorously with a whisk about every 10 minutes to prevent any crystals forming. The ice cream will be finished in about 1 hour 30 minutes.

NUTRITIONAL VALUES PER PORTION:

320 Cal • 6 g protein • 20 g fat • 29 g carbohydrate

Fruity Peach Ice Cream

SERVES 4

300 g (10 oz) peaches (alternatively
nectarines or apricots)

100 g (3$\frac{1}{3}$ oz) dextrose

200 ml (7 fl oz/¾ cup) milk

150 g (5 oz) cream

1 egg yolk

PREPARATION: about 15 mins

CHILLING: about 40 mins

1. Briefly dip the peaches into boiling water, rinse under cold water, then slip off the skins. Halve the peaches and remove the stones. Cut the peach flesh into small dice.

2. Reserve 50 g (1⅔ oz) peach pieces, purée the remaining peaches with the dextrose and milk in the mixer or using a hand-held blender.

3. Whisk together the cream and the egg yolk. Stir into the peach and milk mixture. Fold in the peaches.

4. In the ice cream maker, stir everything for 40 minutes to make a creamy, semi-soft ice cream.

TIP

All three types of ice cream taste best straight from the ice cream maker. If the ice cream is not to be served straightaway, prepare it in a container and store it in the freezer. This will make it rather firm – take it out 30 minutes before serving to soften slighlty.

NUTRITIONAL VALUES PER PORTION:

295 Cal • 4 g protein • 15 g fat • 35 g carbohydrate

Banana Cream with chocolate flakes

SERVES 2

150 g (5 oz) low-fat cream cheese

100 g (3⅓ oz) sour cream

70 g (2½ oz) dextrose

1 banana

30 g (1 oz) dark chocolate
    (70% cocoa)

PREPARATION: about 10 mins

NUTRITIONAL VALUES PER PORTION:

440 Cal • 13 g protein • 18 g fat • 57 g carbohydrate

1. Whisk together the cream cheese, the sour cream and the dextrose.

2. Peel the banana and mash it well with a fork. Fold the banana purée into the cream cheese.

3. Coarsely chop the chocolate. Fill the banana cream into two little bowls and sprinkle the cream with the chocolate.

TIP

Vary the flavour of the cream with seasonal fruits that you can tolerate.

Coconut Cream with papaya

SERVES 2

2 sheets white gelatine

½ vanilla pod

1 packet instant coconut powder
    (alternatively 100 ml/3 fl oz/
    ½ cup coconut milk)

70 g (2½ oz) dextrose

100 g (3⅓ oz) cream

½ pawpaw

PREPARATION: about 30 mins

CHILLING: about 2 hrs

1. Soak the gelatine in cold water for 10 minutes. Slit open the vanilla pod lengthways and scrape out the seeds.

2. In a saucepan, whisk the coconut powder into 100 ml (3 fl oz/½ cup) water per packet instruction and heat through until lukewarm.

3. Squeeze out the gelatine and dissolve in the warm coconut cream. Stir in the vanilla seeds and the dextrose. Chill the cream for about 1 hour, until it starts to set and becomes creamy.

4. Whisk the cream until stiff and fold into the coconut cream. Fill the coconut cream into two dessert bowls and chill in the fridge for about 1 hour or until set.

5. Scrape out the seeds of the papaya and reserve. Peel the fruit and dice the flesh. Sprinkle the papaya and seeds over the coconut cream.

NUTRITIONAL VALUES PER PORTION:

335 Cal • 3 g protein • 16 g fat • 45 g carbohydrate

Almond Cream with an elderflower star

SERVES 2

½ packet vanilla custard powder
(for 500 ml/16 fl oz/2 cups milk)

250 ml (8 fl oz/1 cup) milk

150 g (5 oz) dextrose

60 g (2 oz) ground almonds

50 g (1²/₃ oz) mascarpone

1 level tbsp cornflour (cornstarch)

250 ml (8 fl oz/1 cup)
elderflower juice

PREPARATION: about 40 mins

1. Stir the custard powder into 50 ml (2 fl oz/¼ cup) milk. Bring 200 ml (7 fl oz/¾ cup) milk to the boil with 90 g (3 oz) dextrose. Stir in the custard mixture and briefly bring back to the boil. Fold in the almonds and the mascarpone. Fill the cream into two dessert bowls.

2. Stir the cornflour into 5 tablespoons elderflower juice. Bring the rest of the juice to the boil with 60 g (2 oz) dextrose. Stir in the cornflour mixture. Turn off the heat and leave the cornflour to swell for about 10 minutes.

3. Let the elderflower juice cool slightly. Pour half into the centre of each almond cream. Using a skewer, draw out the liquid to create a star shape.

TIP

This cream also tastes great with 1 tablespoon Toasted Muesli (see page 27).

NUTRITIONAL VALUES PER PORTION:

780 Cal • 12 g protein • 32 g fat • 111 g carbohydrate

Apricots in chocolate

SERVES 2

80 g (2¾ oz) dark chocolate
(70% cocoa)

50 ml (2 fl oz/¼ cup) milk

5 tsp dextrose

6 apricots

200 g (6²/₃ oz) double-cream
cheese

PREPARATION: about 30 mins

1. Break the chocolate into pieces. Heat up the milk with 1 teaspoon dextrose and melt the chocolate in the milk over low heat, stirring constantly.

2. Wash, halve and stone the apricots. Stir together the cream cheese and the rest of the dextrose.

3. Pour the chocolate sauce onto two dessert plates. Place 3 apricot halves on each one. Place dollops of the cream cheese next to the apricots.

VARIATION

If you prefer peaches, bananas or melons, you can simply use these fruits instead, depending on your tolerance.

NUTRITIONAL VALUES PER PORTION:

535 Cal • 14 g protein • 32 g fat • 46 g carbohydrate

Profiteroles with cherries & chocolate cream

MAKES 16 PROFITEROLES
FOR THE DOUGH
100 g (3¹/₃ oz) butter
1 pinch salt
150 g (5 oz) plain flour
4 eggs

FOR THE FILLING
300 g (10 oz) Morello cherries
  (from the jar)
250 g (8 oz) cream
100 g (3¹/₃ oz) dextrose
1 tbsp cocoa
½ tsp cornflour (cornstarch)
30 g (1 oz) dark chocolate
  (70% cocoa)

PLUS
2 tbsp icing sugar
PREPARATION: about 40 mins
BAKING: about 15 mins

1. To make the dough, in a saucepan add 250 ml (8 fl oz/1 cup) water, butter and salt and bring to the boil. Add the flour. Stir vigorously with a wooden spoon for 2 minutes until a ball of dough forms and a thin white residue appears on the base of the pan.

2. Place the dough into a mixing bowl. Using the kneading hook of a hand-held blender, stir in the eggs one at a time, until the dough becomes shiny.

3. Preheat the oven to 225°C/200°C fan-forced (middle shelf). Line a baking tray with baking paper. Fill the dough into a piping bag with a large nozzle. Pipe 16 rosettes of about 6 cm (2½ in) diameter onto the tray, leaving 5 cm (2 in) space in between them.

4. Bake the profiteroles in the oven for about 15 minutes. Take them out and, using scissors, cut off the top third of each profiterole. Leave to cool completely.

5. To make the filling, drain the cherries. Whisk the cream with the dextrose, cocoa and cornflour until stiff. Finely chop the chocolate and fold in.

6. Place one dollop of chocolate cream on each bottom profiterole half. Divide the cherries between them and loosely cover with the tops. Dust the profiteroles with icing sugar.

TIP
If you haven't got a piping bag, you can simply shape the dough heaps using two tablespoons.

VARIATION
The profiteroles are also delicious when filled with Chocolate and Vanilla Cherry Cream (see page 31). Or why not try a mixture of whipped cream and banana slices? Or if you prefer fill the profiteroles with vanilla custard (sweetened with dextrose) or with a Nut & Nougat Cream (see page 32).

NUTRITIONAL VALUES PER PORTION:
195 Cal • 3 g protein • 12 g fat • 17 g carbohydrate

Marbled Berry Cake

**MAKES 12 PIECES
(1 LOOSE-BOTTOMED TIN,
26 CM/10 IN DIAMETER)**

FOR THE BASE

butter, for greasing

flour, for dusting

4 eggs

160 g (5¹/₃ oz) dextrose

120 g (4 oz) cornflour (cornstarch)

120 g (4 oz) plain flour

1 tsp baking powder

FOR THE YOGHURT CREAM

7 sheets white gelatine

1 tbsp lemon juice

50 g (1²/₃ oz) sugar

100 g (3¹/₃ oz) dextrose

500 g (1 lb) natural yoghurt

200 g (6½ oz) cream

FOR THE FRUIT PURÉE

300 g (10 oz) mixed berries
   (fresh or frozen)

60 g (2 oz) dextrose

1 tsp liquid sweetener

3 sheets white gelatine

extra berries for decorating

PREPARATION: about 20 mins

BAKING: about 35 mins

CHILLING: about 4 hrs

1. Preheat the oven to 170°C/160°C fan-forced (middle shelf). Grease the base of a baking tin and dust with flour. Using a hand-held blender, beat the eggs with 4 tablespoons water until thick and foamy. Gradually add the dextrose, continuing to beat at the highest setting. Sift the cornflour, flour and baking powder onto the dough and carefully fold in.

2. Place the base in the baking tin and bake for about 35 minutes. Leave to cool a little, then remove from the tin and cool completely on a cake rack.

3. To make the yoghurt cream, soak the gelatine in cold water. Stir the lemon juice, sugar and dextrose into the yoghurt. Squeeze out the gelatine and dissolve in a small saucepan over low heat. Stir in 3 tablespoons yoghurt cream, then the remaining yoghurt cream.

4. Chill the yoghurt cream for about 15 minutes until it starts to set. Beat the cream until stiff, then fold carefully into the yoghurt cream. Now spread the cream mixture evenly on top of the pastry base.

5. To make the fruit purée, carefully wash and trim or pick over the berries, leave to drain. If using frozen berries, leave to thaw. Finely purée the berries in a mixer or with a hand-held blender. Pass the purée through a fine sieve, then stir in the dextrose and the sweetener.

6. Soak the gelatine in cold water. Lightly squeeze it out, then dissolve in a small saucepan over low heat. First combine with 3 tablespoons fruit purée, then stir the mixture into the remaining fruit purée.

7. Spread the fruit purée on top of the yoghurt cream and use a fork to decorate the cake in a spiral pattern. Chill the cake for about 4 hours before serving. Serve with extra berries on top.

NUTRITIONAL VALUES PER PORTION:
305 Cal • 7 g protein • 9 g fat • 50 g carbohydrate

Sour Cream Slice

**MAKES 16 PIECES
(1 DEEP BAKING TRAY)**

FOR THE BASE

butter, for greasing

flour, for dusting

250 g (8 oz) butter

220 g (7 oz) dextrose

1 egg

460 g (15 oz) plain flour

4 tsp baking powder

1 tsp cinnamon

FOR THE TOPPING

750 g (1½ lb) low-fat
  cream cheese

250 g (8 oz) sour cream

½ packet vanilla custard powder
  (for 500 ml/16 fl oz/
  2 cups milk)

1 egg

200 g (6½ oz) dextrose

8 drops lemon essence (alternatively
  1 tbsp lemon juice)

PREPARATION: about 40 mins

BAKING: about 45 mins

1. Preheat the oven to 170°C/150°C fan-forced (middle shelf). Grease a baking tray, then dust with flour.

2. Beat the butter with the dextrose until pale. Stir in the egg. Sift the flour and the baking powder on top of the dough and stir in briefly. Spread two-thirds of the base on the baking tray, forming a 2 cm (¾ in) rim. Press down firmly.

3. To make the topping, whisk together the cream cheese, sour cream and custard powder. Stir in the egg, dextrose and lemon essence. Spread the cream on top of the base.

4. Stir the cinnamon into the remaining third of the base. Break the cinnamon mixture into short pieces and distribute these on top of the cake.

5. Bake the slice in the oven for about 45 minutes until golden.

ARTIFICIAL FLAVOURS

During the abstention phase you should only use artificial lemon flavourings in your cakes. Such flavourings are usually sold in small tubes or bottles which allow you to use a drop at a time. They are sold in the baking departments. During the test phase you can start to try freshly squeezed juice or the grated zest of organic lemons.

NUTRITIONAL VALUES PER PORTION:
405 Cal • 11 g protein • 18 g fat • 50 g carbohydrate

Butter Cake with almonds

MAKES 16 PIECES
(1 DEEP BAKING TRAY)

1 cube fresh yeast (42 g/1½ oz),
  alternatively 3 tsp dried yeast)
500 g (1 lb) plain flour
220 g (7 oz) dextrose
1 egg, 1 pinch salt
250 ml (8 fl oz/1 cup)
  lukewarm milk
butter, for greasing
flour, for dusting
150 g (5 oz) soft butter
150 g (5 oz) flaked almonds

PREPARATION: about 10 mins
RESTING: about 60 mins
BAKING: about 15 mins

NUTRITIONAL VALUES PER PORTION:
300 Cal • 6 g protein • 14 g fat • 36 g carbohydrate

1. Crumble the yeast into a bowl. Add the flour, 120 g (4 oz) dextrose, the egg and salt, and whisk together using a hand-held blender. Gradually add the milk and continue whisking on the lowest setting, until you have a smooth dough. Cover and leave to rise in a warm place for about 30 minutes.

2. Grease a baking tray and dust with flour. Knead the dough once more and leave to rest again for about 10 minutes. With moistened hands, spread the dough evenly on the tray.

3. Divide the butter into small pats and distribute these evenly on the dough. Sprinkle over the almonds and 100 g (3⅓ oz) dextrose. Leave to rest again for about 20 minutes, until the cake has clearly risen. Preheat the oven to 220°C/200°C fan-forced (middle shelf).

4. Bake the cake in the oven for about 15 minutes until it is golden all over.

Cinnamon Waffles

MAKES 8-10 WAFFLES

1 vanilla pod
125 g (4 oz) soft butter
140 g (4½ oz) dextrose
2 tsp cinnamon
2 tsp orange flavour (alternatively
  grated zest of an organic orange)
3 eggs
125 g (4 oz) cream
120 ml (4 fl oz/½ cup) milk
250 g (8 oz) plain flour
1 tsp baking powder
butter, for greasing
dextrose, for dusting

PREPARATION: about 35 mins

1. Slit the vanilla pod open lengthways and scrape out the seeds. Beat with the butter, dextrose, cinnamon and orange flavour until pale. Stir in the eggs, one at a time. Stir in the cream and the milk. Sift the flour and the baking powder onto the dough. Stir everything to form a thick, liquid batter. Leave to rest for 10 minutes.

2. Preheat the waffle iron to a medium setting. Lightly grease both baking surfaces. Place 3 tablespoons batter in the middle of the lower baking area and close the iron. Bake the waffles, one at a time, for about 2–3 minutes until golden. Place on a wire rack to cool a little.

3. Continue until all the batter has been used up. Lightly dust the waffles with a little dextrose before serving.

SERVE WITH

During the abstention phase you can enjoy a tasty fruit spread (see pages 30-31) or a Chocolate Butter (see page 32) with the waffles. During the test phase you could serve a compote of blueberries, cherries or other types of fruit that you can tolerate as toppings.

NUTRITIONAL VALUES PER PORTION:
300 Cal • 5 g protein • 17 g fat • 33 g carbohydrate

Hazelnut Coffee Cake

**MAKES 16 PIECES
(1 LOAF TIN, 30 CM/12 IN)**

250 g (8 oz) ground hazelnuts

250 g (8 oz) plain flour

4 tsp baking powder

270 g (9½ oz) dextrose

4 drops almond extract

100 ml (3 fl oz/½ cup) milk

about 140 ml (4½ fl oz/⅔ cup)
strong cold coffee

butter, for greasing

flour, or dusting

PREPARATION: about 10 mins

BAKING: about 50 mins

1. Preheat the oven to 200°C/180°C fan-forced (middle shelf). Combine the nuts with the flour, baking powder and 220 g (7 oz) dextrose. Using a hand-held blender, stir in the almond extract, milk and coffee, until the mixture starts to stick to a spoon.

2. Grease the loaf tin and dust with flour. Place the batter in the tin and bake in the oven for 50 minutes until golden.

3. Once slightly cooled, remove the cake from the tin and place on a cake rack to cool completely. Before serving, dust with the remaining dextrose.

TIP
This cake is like a loaf of bread in texture. If you prefer something lighter, just stir 2 eggs into the mixture when you are adding the coffee.

NUTRITIONAL VALUES PER PORTION:
225 Cal • 4 g protein • 10 g fat • 30 g carbohydrate

Apricot Slice with almond brittle

**MAKES 20 PIECES
(1 DEEP BAKING TRAY)**

butter, for greasing

flour, for dusting

6 eggs

420 g (14 oz) dextrose

180 g (5¾ oz) plain flour

180 g (5¾ oz) cornflour (cornstarch)

1 tsp baking powder

2 large tins apricots (465 g/
15 oz each drained weight)

2 packets vanilla custard powder (for
500 ml/16 fl oz/2 cups milk)

800 ml (28 fl oz/3½ cups) milk
(1.5% fat)

500 g (1 lb) low-fat cream cheese

50 g (1²/₃ oz) flaked almonds

1-2 tbsp sugar

PREPARATION: about 20 mins

BAKING: about 30 mins

1. Preheat the oven to 180°C/160°C fan-forced (middle shelf). Grease a baking tray and dust with flour. Using a hand-held blender, beat the eggs with 6 tablespoons water until thick and foamy. Gradually add 240 g (8 oz) dextrose, continuing to whisk at the highest setting. Sift the flour, cornflour and baking powder onto the mixture and carefully fold them in.

2. Spread the dough evenly on the baking tray and bake in the oven for about 30 minutes.

3. Meanwhile, drain the apricots. Stir the custard powder into 200 ml (7 fl oz/¾ cup) milk. In a saucepan, bring 600 ml (20 fl oz/2½ cups) milk and 180 g (5¾ oz) dextrose to the boil. Stir in the custard powder and milk mixture and briefly bring to the boil. Take the custard off the heat; leave to cool for 5 minutes.

4. Once slightly cooled, remove the cake from the baking tray and transfer to a cake rack to cool completely.

5. Pat the apricot halves dry with kitchen paper. Place them on the pastry base, cut surface down. Fold the cream cheese into the custard, then spread on top of the apricots. Leave to cool.

6. Dry-roast the almond flakes and the sugar in a non-stick pan without fat over low heat, stirring constantly, until the sugar has caramelised. Sprinkle the almond brittle over the cake.

NUTRITIONAL VALUES PER PORTION:
265 Cal • 8 g protein • 4 g fat • 50 g carbohydrate

Old-fashioned Cheesecake

MAKES 16 PIECES
(1 BAKING TRAY)

250 g (8 oz) plain flour

125 g (4 oz) soft butter

4 tbsp + 210 g (7 oz) dextrose

5 eggs

1 vanilla pod

200 g (6½ oz) margarine

750 g (1½ lb) low-fat cream cheese

6 tbsp fine semolina

5 drops lemon flavour (alternatively ½
   tsp grated zest of an organic lemon)

4 tsp baking powder

butter, for greasing

flour, for dusting

PREPARATION: about 15 mins

NUTRITIONAL VALUES PER PORTION:
345 Cal • 10 g protein • 19 g fat • 33 g carbohydrate

BAKING: about 55 mins

1. Using the kneading hook of a hand-held blender, knead the flour and the butter. Add 4 tablespoons dextrose, 1 egg and 2 tablespoons water and knead until you have a smooth dough. Shape the dough into a flattened roll, then wrap in cling film and chill in the fridge.

2. Slit the vanilla pod open lengthways and scrape out the seeds. Beat the margarine until pale, then gradually stir in the cream cheese and 210 g (7 oz) dextrose. Stir in 4 eggs, one at a time. Stir in the semolina, the lemon flavour, the vanilla seeds and the baking powder.

3. Preheat the oven to 180°C/160°C fan-forced (middle shelf). Grease a baking tray and dust with flour. Roll out the dough on a work surface dusted with flour, then transfer to the tray. Shape a 2 cm (¾ in) high rim.

4. Spread the cream cheese mixture onto the base. Bake in the oven for about 55 minutes until golden.

Poppyseed Crumble Cake

MAKES 16 PIECES
(1 BAKING TRAY)

1 cube fresh yeast (42 g/1½ oz,
   alternatively 4 tsp dried yeast)

575 g (1 lb 2 oz) plain flour

570 g (1 lb 2 oz) dextrose

1 tsp lemon flavour
   (alternatively grated zest
   of an organic lemon)

180 ml (6½ fl oz/¾ cup) warm milk

275 g (9½ oz) soft butter

butter, for greasing

flour, for dusting

1¼ l (50 fl oz/6 cups) milk

125 g (4 oz) coarse-grain semolina

375 g (12 oz) ground poppy seeds

2 tbsp cinnamon

PREPARATION: about 35 mins

RISING: about 50 mins

BAKING: about 45 mins

1. To make the base, crumble the yeast and combine with 375 g (12 oz) flour, 130 g (4¼ oz) dextrose and the lemon flavour. With the dough hooks of a hand-held blender, knead in the milk and 75 g (2¾ oz) butter.

2. Preheat the oven to 50°C/50°C fan-forced (middle shelf). Turn off the heat. Cover and place the dough in the oven to rise for 30 minutes. Grease a baking tray and dust it with flour.

3. Knead the dough again and spread evenly with your hands on the tray. Place in the warm oven to rise for 20 minutes.

4. For the topping, bring the milk to the boil with 240 g (8 oz) dextrose. Add the semolina and the poppy seeds and bring back to the boil, stirring constantly. Turn off the heat and leave the poppy seeds to swell for 15 minutes. Spread the poppy mixture onto the dough. Preheat the oven to 200°C/180°C fan-forced (middle shelf).

5. To make the crumble knead together 200 g (6½ oz) flour, 200 g (6½ oz) butter, 200 g (6½ oz) dextrose and the cinnamon. Spread evenly on the poppy cake and bake in the oven for about 45 minutes until crunchy and golden.

NUTRITIONAL VALUES PER PORTION:
590 Cal • 13 g protein • 28 g fat • 72 g carbohydrate

Orange & Chocolate Cake

MAKES 16 PIECES
(1 LOAF TIN, 30 CM/12 IN)

1 vanilla pod

125 g (4 oz) margarine

450 g (15 oz) dextrose

3 eggs

250 g (8 oz) plain flour

75 g (2¾ oz) cocoa

2 tsp baking powder

150 g (5 oz) cream

2 tsp orange flavour
(alternatively grated zest
of an organic orange)

butter, for greasing

flour, for dusting

PREPARATION: about 10 mins

BAKING: about 60 mins
RESTING: about 12 hrs

1. Slit open the vanilla pod lengthways and scrape out the seeds. Beat with the margarine and 290 g (10 oz) dextrose until foamy. Stir in the eggs, one at a time. Stir in the flour, 45 g (1½ oz) cocoa and baking powder. Add the cream and orange flavour.

2. Preheat the oven to 175°C/160°C fan-forced (middle shelf). Grease the baking tin and dust with flour. Place the dough into the tin and bake for 60 minutes. Cool a little, turn out and leave to cool on a cake rack.

3. To make the icing, whisk 160 g (5⅓ oz) dextrose, 30 g (1 oz) cocoa and 4 tablespoons hot water; stir into the mix.

4. Ice the cake with the icing and leave to dry for at least 12 hours or overnight.

TIP

The icing keeps the cake moist and fresh. Alternatively you could make a glaze instead – see recipe on page 123.

NUTRITIONAL VALUES PER PORTION:
300 Cal • 4 g protein • 13 g fat • 41 g carbohydrate

Mixed Fruit Tart

MAKES 12 PIECES
(1 LOOSE-BOTTOMED TIN,
26 CM/10 IN DIAMETER)

butter, for greasing

flour, for dusting

4 eggs

160 g (5⅓ oz) + 3 tbsp dextrose

120 g (4 oz) cornflour (cornstarch)

120 g (4 oz) plain flour

1 tsp baking powder

2 bananas

2 kiwi fruit

100 g (3⅓ oz) berries (raspberries,
blueberries, blackberries)

½ papaya (100 g/3⅓ oz,
if desired)

250 g (8 oz) apricot jam

PREPARATION: about 65 mins
BAKING: about 35 mins

1. Preheat the oven to 175°C/160°C fan-forced (middle shelf). Grease the bottom of a baking tin and dust with flour.

2. Using a hand-held blender, beat the eggs with 4 tablespoons water until thick and foamy. Gradually add 160 g (5⅓ oz) dextrose, continuing to beat at the highest setting. Sift cornflour, flour and baking powder onto the dough and gently fold in.

3. Press the dough into the tin and bake in the oven for 35 minutes. Leave to cool a little; transfer to a cake rack to cool completely.

4. Peel the bananas and kiwi fruit and cut into 1 cm (½ in) thick slices. Carefully wash and pat dry the berries. Peel the papaya if using and scrape out the seeds. Cut into strips and arrange on the pastry base.

5. Melt the jam in a bowl set over a saucepan with gently simmering water. Brush over the tart and chill in the fridge to set.

NUTRITIONAL VALUES PER PORTION:
185 Cal • 3 g protein • 2 g fat • 39 g carbohydrate

Sweet Shortcrust Pastry

**MAKES 12 PIECES
(1 LOOSE-BOTTOM TIN,
26 CM/10 IN DIAMETER)**

150 g (5 oz) margarine

1 egg

300 g (10 oz) plain flour

180 g (5¾ oz) dextrose

1 pinch salt

1 tsp lemon flavour
(alternatively grated zest
of an organic lemon)

PREPARATION: about 10 mins

CHILLING: about 30 mins

BAKING: about 20 mins

1. Using the kneading hook of a hand-held blender, combine the margarine and the egg until foamy. Gradually stir in the flour. Add the dextrose, salt and lemon flavour and knead until you have a smooth dough, adding a little water if needed.

2. Shape the dough into a shallow disc, wrap in cling film and chill for about 30 minutes.

3. Preheat the oven to 200°C/180°C fan-forced (middle shelf). Press the dough into the tin, forming a 2 cm (¾ in) rim. Bake in the oven for about 20 minutes until golden.

BAKING WITH DEXTROSE

If the cake is to have a pastry top, just bake twice the amount. For biscuits, roll out the dough to 3 mm thick, cut out shapes as desired and place them on a baking tray. Bake as per the recipe for about 10 minutes or until golden. For cakes with toppings and fillings, simply replace the amount of sugar given in the recipes to the ratio of 1:1.3 with dextrose.

NUTRITIONAL VALUES PER PORTION:
245 Cal • 3 g protein • 11 g fat • 33 g carbohydrate

Sponge Cake

**MAKES 12 PIECES
(1 RING CAKE TIN, 1.5 LITRES/
60 FL OZ/7½ CUPS)**

butter, for greasing

flour, for dusting

1 vanilla pod

250 g (8 oz) margarine

300 g (10 oz) dextrose

1 pinch salt

4 eggs

500 g (1 lb) plain flour

4 tsp baking powder

about 170 ml (6 fl oz/¾ cup) milk

PREPARATION: about 15 mins

BAKING: about 60 mins

1. Grease the baking tin; dust with flour. Slit vanilla pod open lengthways; scrape out seeds.

2. Preheat the oven to 170°C/150°C fan-forced (bottom shelf). Beat the margarine and the dextrose together until pale. Add the vanilla seeds and the salt. Stir in the eggs, one at a time. Sift the flour and the baking powder onto the batter, then fold in. Add as much milk as needed to make the batter drop sloppily off a spoon.

3. Pour the batter into the tin and bake for 60 minutes. Cool a little, then remove from the tin.

TIP

The dextrose will make the dough crispier than you may be used to. It is therefore better to bake at a slightly lower temperature.

VARIATION

To make a Marble Cake fill two-thirds of the batter into the baking tin. Combine the remaining third with 30 g (1 oz) cocoa and 2-3 tablespoons milk. Spread on top of the light batter. Create spiral shapes using a fork. Bake as per the recipe.

NUTRITIONAL VALUES PER PORTION:

430 Cal • 7 g protein • 20 g fat • 56 g carbohydrate

Sponge Cake Base

**MAKES 12 PIECES
(1 LOOSE-BOTTOMED TIN,
26 CM/10 IN DIAMETER)**

butter, for greasing

flour, for dusting

1 vanilla pod

4 eggs

160 g (5⅓ oz) dextrose

2 tsp lemon flavour (alternatively
grated zest of an organic lemon)

1 pinch cinnamon

120 g (4 oz) cornflour (cornstarch)

120 g (4 oz) plain flour

1 tsp baking powder

PREPARATION: about 20 mins

BAKING: about 35 mins

1. Preheat the oven to 175°C/160°C fan-forced (middle shelf). Grease the bottom of a baking tin and thinly dust with flour, do not cover the rim. Slit the vanilla pod open lengthways and scrape out the seeds.

2. Using a hand-held blender, beat the eggs and 4 tablespoons water until thick and foamy. Gradually add the dextrose, continuing to beat at the highest setting. Stir in the lemon flavour, cinnamon and vanilla seeds. Sift the cornflour, flour and baking powder onto the dough and carefully fold in.

3. Fill the dough into the baking tin and bake the pastry base for about 35 minutes in the oven.

4. Once cooled a little, remove the base from the tin and place on a cake rack to cool completely.

TIP

During the abstention phase, you can cover the sponge base with a cream cheese or yoghurt cream. During the test phase you can also top with a variety of fruits that you can tolerate.

NUTRITIONAL VALUES PER PORTION:

150 Cal • 3 g protein • 2 g fat • 30 g carbohydrate

Chocolate Cornflake Cakes

MAKES 25 PIECES

60 g (2 oz) almond slivers

125 g (4 oz) butter

1½ tbsp dextrose

2 tbsp cocoa

50 g (1²/₃ oz) cornflakes

PREPARATION: about 20 mins

1. Dry-roast the almond slivers in a non-stick frying pan without fat until golden. Place on a plate to cool completely.

2. In a saucepan, melt the butter with the dextrose and the cocoa over low heat, then turn off the heat.

3. Stir the almond slivers and the cornflakes into the chocolate mixture.

4. Line a baking tray with baking paper and place little heaps of the mixture on top, using two teaspoons. Leave to cool before serving.

NUTRITIONAL VALUES PER PORTION:

65 Cal • 1 g protein • 6 g fat • 3 g carbohydrate

Muesli Biscuits

MAKES 80 PIECES

125 g (4 oz) soft butter, 2 eggs

120 g (4 oz) dextrose

150 g (5 oz) instant oats

25 g (¾ oz) coconut flakes

50 g (1²/₃ oz) ground almonds

1 pinch cinnamon

100 g (3¹/₃ oz) wholemeal spelt flour

25 g (¾ oz) sunflower seeds

PREPARATION: about 20 mins

BAKING: about 20 mins

1. Preheat the oven to 200°C/180°C fan-forced (middle shelf). Line a baking tray with baking paper. Beat the butter with the eggs until foamy. Stir in the dextrose. Using the kneading hook of a hand-held blender, stir in the oats, coconut flakes, almonds, cinnamon, flour and seeds.

2. Shape the dough into a long roll (4 cm/1½ in diameter) and cut into 1 cm (½ in) slices. Place on the tray and bake in the oven for about 20 minutes. Leave to cool.

NUTRITIONAL VALUES PER PORTION:

40 Cal • 1 g protein • 2 g fat • 3 g carbohydrate

Nut & Almond Brittle

MAKES 15 PIECES

50 g (1²/₃ oz) chopped hazelnuts

50 g (1²/₃ oz) chopped almonds

100 g (3¹/₃ oz) dextrose

PREPARATION: about 10 mins

1. Dry-roast the nuts, almonds and dextrose in a non-stick pan on low heat for 5–8 minutes, stirring constantly, until the sugar has caramelised.

2. Line a baking tray with baking paper. Spread the nut mixture onto the tray and leave to cool. Break the brittle into smaller pieces.

VARIATION

You can also make these tasty treats with walnuts, cashew nuts or desiccated coconut for a change. The brittle will keep for about 4 weeks if stored in a well-sealed tin.

NUTRITIONAL VALUES PER PORTION:

65 Cal • 1 g protein • 4 g fat • 7 g carbohydrate

Dark Glaze

FOR 1 CAKE

90 g (3 oz) coconut fat

120 g (4 oz) dextrose

60 g (2 oz) cocoa

1-2 tbsp cream

1 tsp vanilla essence

PREPARATION: about 35 mins

RESTING: about 12 hrs

1. Melt the coconut fat in a bowl over a saucepan of simmering water. Mix the dextrose and cocoa in a separate bowl.

2. Using a hand-held blender on low speed, whisk the cocoa sugar and the melted coconut fat. Add cream and vanilla and continue beating for at least 3 minutes.

3. Use the glaze immediately. If required, reheat again in a bowl over a saucepan with simmering water. Leave to dry for 12 hours.

TIP

The longer you stir the ingredients, the smoother and shinier the glaze will be and the richer it will taste.

NUTRITIONAL VALUES PER PORTION:

1535 Cal • 16 g protein • 106 g fat • 131 g carbohydrate

	DIET PHASE 1 ABSTENTION PHASE	**DIET PHASE 2** TEST PHASE
BREAKFAST, SPREADS AND DRINKS	banana & coconut cream (p. 33) breakfast bake (p. 37) cheesy butter (p. 34) chocolate butter (p. 32) delicious white bread (p. 28) eggs and toast with spinach (p. 37) nut & nougat cream (p. 32) oatmeal muesli (p. 26) Parmesan & egg spread (p. 35) salmon butter* (p. 35) seaside breakfast (p. 36) sweet almond spread (p. 33) toasted muesli (p. 27) vanilla buttermilk with wheat bran (p. 39) yoghurt bread (p. 28)	apricot spread (p. 31) berry jam (p. 30) blueberry smoothie (p. 38) grapefruit drink with cherry ice (p. 38) oatmeal muesli (p. 26) peach & kiwi fruit punch (p. 39) red basil butter (p. 34) vanilla cherry cream (p. 31) 
CAKES AND BAKING	butter cake (p. 112) chocolate cornflake cakes (p. 122) cinnamon waffles (p. 112) dark glaze (p. 123) hazelnut coffee cake (p. 114) muesli biscuits (p. 122) old-fashioned cheesecake (p. 116) nut & almond brittle (p. 123) orange & chocolate cake (p. 118) poppyseed crumble cake (p. 116) sour cream slice (p. 110) sponge cake (p. 121) sponge cake base (p. 121) sweet shortcrust pastry (p. 120)	apricot slice w. almond brittle (p. 114) marbled berry cake (p. 108) mixed fruit tart (p. 118) profiteroles with cherries and chocolate (p. 106) 
SALADS	carrot salad with toasted cashew nuts* (p. 46) cucumber & tomato salad (p. 40) feta & pasta salad* (p. 42) fresh cheese salad (p. 42) peanut & sesame sauce (p. 49) thousand island dressing (p. 48) yoghurt salad cream* (p. 49)	Asian chicken salad (p. 44) nutty fennel & kiwi salad (p. 44) sweetcorn salad with tuna and tomato (p. 40)

*= can also be prepared without the use of onion and garlic

DIET PHASE 1
ABSTENTION PHASE

cream of pumpkin soup (p. 50)
curried banana soup* (p. 52)
ham & olive balls (p. 56)
pancake wraps w. ham & olives* (p. 54)
potato & ham muffins* (p. 60)
potato soup with salmon* (p. 50)
tomato dip* (p. 56)
vegetable & Swiss cheese
  carpaccio (p. 58)
yoghurt & avocado cream (p. 59)

baked salmon with herbs (p. 72)
broccoli flan (p. 62)
colourful meatloaf (p. 80)
crunchy meat patties* (p. 86)
fillet parcels with prosciutto and
  melted cheese (p. 84)
fluffy potato bake (p. 64)
Italian-style tomato chicken* (p. 74)
ling fish on mustard vegetables (p. 72)
pork fillet on vegetables* (p. 82)
ribbon pasta with mushrooms
  and pine nuts* (p. 66)
risi e bisi (p. 70)
spinach lasagne* (p. 66)
spinach with gorgonzola cream* (p. 64)
turkey & vegetable kebabs (p. 78)
veggie rice with cashew nuts (p. 70)

almond cream with an elderflower
  star (p. 104)
banana cream w. chocolate flakes (p. 102)
bananas in chocolate chilli
  sauce (p. 98)
chocolate ice cream (p. 100)
cream cheese blinis (p. 92)
creamy vanilla ice cream (p. 101)
rhubarb compote with vanilla (p. 96)

DIET PHASE 2
TEST PHASE

curried orange dip (p. 59)
vegetable soup (p. 52)
vegetable waffles (p. 60)

**SOUPS AND
SNACKS**

baked chicken breast with herbed
  potatoes* (p. 76)
beef stir-fry with snowpeas (p. 88)
ginger and turkey pot with herbs* (p. 78)
meaty Mexican tortillas (p. 68)

**MAIN
COURSES**

apricots in chocolate (p. 104)
coconut cream with papaya (p. 102)
fruity peach ice cream (p. 100)
melon cocktail with cinnamon
  cream cheese (p. 98)
raspberries with mascarpone
  and pine nuts (p. 90)
semolina pudding with kiwi fruit (p. 96)
sweet donuts with cherry sauce (p. 92)
yoghurt mousse with berry sauce (p. 94)

DESSERTS

FOOD	FRUCTOSE (g/100 g food)	GLUCOSE (g/100 g food)	RATIO fructose/ glucose	SORBITOL (g/100 g food)
FRUIT				
apple	5.74	2.03	2.83	0.52
apple, dried	27.80	9.80	2.84	2.49
apricot	0.87	1.73	0.50	0.82
apricot, dried	4.88	9.69	0.50	4.60
avocado	0.20	0.10	2.00	*
banana	3.40	3.55	0.96	*
blackberry	3.11	2.96	1.05	*
blueberries	3.34	2.47	1.35	*
cherries, morello	4.28	5.18	0.83	*
cherries, sweet	6.30	7.13	0.88	*
cranberries	2.93	3.03	0.97	*
date	24.90	25.00	1.00	1.35
fig, dried	23.50	25.70	0.91	*
gooseberries	3.33	3.02	1.10	*
grapefruit	2.10	2.38	0.88	*
grapes	7.08	7.10	1.00	0.20
honeydew melon	1.30	1.60	0.81	*
kiwi fruit	4.59	4.32	1.06	*
lemon	1.35	1.40	0.96	*
lime	0.80	0.80	1.00	*
lychee	3.20	5.00	0.64	*
mandarin	1.30	1.70	0.76	*
mango	2.60	0.85	3.06	*
mirabelle plum	4.30	5.10	0.84	*
orange	2.58	2.29	1.13	*
passion fruit	2.81	3.64	0.77	*
pawpaw	3.50	3.60	0.97	*
peach	1.23	1.04	1.18	0.89
pear	6.73	1.67	4.03	2.17
pineapple	2.44	2.13	1.15	*
pineapple, tinned	5.2	5.2	1.00	*
plum	2.01	3.36	0.60	1.41
plum, dried (prune)	9.37	15.70	0.60	6.57
pomegranate	7.90	7.20	1.10	*
raisins	33.20	32.00	1.04	0.89

FOOD	FRUCTOSE (g/100 g food)	GLUCOSE (g/100 g food)	RATIO fructose/ glucose	SORBITOL (g/100 g food)
raspberries	2.05	1.75	1.17	0.01
rhubarb	0.39	0.41	0.95	*
rosehips	7.30	7.30	1.00	*
strawberry	2.24	2.17	1.03	0.03
watermelon	3.92	2.02	1.94	*
VEGETABLES				
broccoli	0.80	0.75	1.07	*
carrots	1.30	1.40	0.93	*
cauliflower	0.76	0.88	0.86	*
kohlrabi	1.23	1.39	0.88	*
sweetcorn	0.38	0.62	0.61	*
DRINKS				
apple juice	6.40	2.40	2.67	0.56
coke drinks	2.08	2.85	0.73	*
lager beer, light	*	0.013	*	0.002
malt beer	0.25	0.38	0.66	*
orange juice	2.47	2.61	0.95	*
red wine, dry	0.25	0.31	0.81	0.01
white wine, dry	0.41	0.38	1.08	0.01

* = no data available

SOURCES: Souci, Fachmann, Kraut (www.sfk-online.net, August 2006)
The figures listed here give average values which will vary depending on the particular variety chosen and by their degree of ripeness.

EXPLANATION

If the ratio is < 1 (smaller than 1), the food contains more glucose than fructose. These foods are ofen better tolerated. Aside from the glucose-fructose ratio the total quantity of sugar also plays an important role. A food that has an altogether very high fructose content, for example dried figs, can lead to an intolerance quite independent from the glucose content. An altogether low fructose content, such as that of avocado, will generally not lead to symptoms despite having an unfavourable glucose-fructose ratio. You are generally advised to avoid all the foods printed in bold since these will almost always cause discomfort.

GOOD TO KNOW

BOOKS, ADDRESSES AND LINKS FOR FURTHER HELP

If you are suffering from any of the symptoms listed in this book, you are strongly advised to have yourself diagnosed rather than undergoing self-diagnosis. Make sure your GP sends you for a breath test, then consult a dietitian to help you find the right diet for your individual disorders and intolerances.

BOOKS AND FURTHER INFORMATION

Shepherd Works
http://shepherdworks.com.au/disease-information/fructose-malabsorption
A private website with useful information on the subject of fructose malabsorption.

Foodintol
www.foodintol.com
A campaigning website run by Deborah Manners who is not a doctor or dietitian but has suffered from food intolerances for years and now runs this information site for the benefit of fellow-sufferers.

Fructose and me
www.fructoseandme.com
This is another website run by a fructose malabsorption sufferer who shares her research, information, tips and recipes with fellow sufferers.

Useful books
Jill Thomas, *Healthy Gut Guide: Natural Solutions for Your Digestive Disorders.* London: Penguin, 2007.
Debra Ledford and Bob Ledford, *Fructose Malabsorption.* Brookings, OR: Ledford Publishing, 2009.

RECIPE INDEX - BY CHAPTER

INDEX

This edition published in 2015 by New Holland Publishers Pty Ltd
London • Sydney • Auckland

Unit 9, The Chandlery, 50 Westminster Bridge Road, London SE1 7QY, United Kingdom
1/66 Gibbes Street, Chatswood, NSW 2067, Australia
218 Lake Road, Northcote, Auckland 0627, New Zealand

www.newhollandpublishers.com

Published originally under the title Lower Your Fructose by Anne Kamp and Christiane Schäfer
ISBN 3-8338-0650, © 2007 Gräfe und Unzer Verlag GmbH, München (ISBN 3-7742-6650) © 2004 by GRÄFE UND
UNZER VERLAG GmbH, München
English translation copyright: © 2012 by Silva Editions Ltd., France.

A record of this book is held at the British Library and the National Library of Australia.
ISBN 9781742574738

DISCLAIMER: The nutritional information for each recipe is an estimate only and may vary depending on the brand of
ingredients used and due to natural biological variations in the composition of natural foods such as meat, fish, fruit and
vegetables. All information provided in this book is intended to be a guide only, it does not replace medical advice. Any
concerns readers have about their diet should be discussed with their doctor. Whilst all reasonable efforts have been made
to ensure the accuracy of the information, the Publisher accepts no responsibility for the accuracy of that information or
for any error or omission and shall not be responsible for any decisions made based on such information.

Managing Director: Fiona Schultz
Publisher: Alan Whiticker
Project Editor: Angela Sutherland
Designer: Thomas Casey
Production Director: Olga Dementiev
Printer: Toppan Leefung Printing Ltd

10 9 8 7 6 5 4 3 2 1

Keep up with New Holland Publishers on Facebook
www.facebook.com/NewHollandPublishers